Water from the Well

Water
from the
Well

❧ SARAH, REBEKAH,
RACHEL, AND LEAH ❧

―――――

Anne Roiphe

wm
WILLIAM MORROW
An Imprint of HarperCollins*Publishers*

HarperCollins books may be purchased for educational, business, or sales promotional use. For information please write: Special Markets Department, HarperCollins Publishers, 10 East 53rd Street, New York, NY 10022.

FIRST EDITION

Designed by Susan Yang

Library of Congress Cataloging-in-Publication Data has been applied for.

ISBN-13: 978-0-06-073796-2
ISBN-10: 0-06-073796-4

06   07   08   09   10   WBC/RRD   10   9   8   7   6   5   4   3   2   1

*To Benjamin Gruenstein
and his daughter Ella*

ACKNOWLEDGMENTS

I want to thank my husband, Dr. Herman Roiphe, for his own psychoanalytic work on the book of Genesis, which sparked my interest in the world of the Bible. I want to thank him for the many conversations we had on this subject. I want to thank him for all the other ideas and thoughts he gave me over the thirty-nine years of our marriage.

I thank Rabbi Adin Steinsaltz for giving me some of his time, and I thank the Joint Distribution Committee, and in particular Amir Shaviv for helping me to visit the burial places of Abraham and Sarah, Jacob and Leah and Rachel.

I am very grateful to the librarians of the Jewish Theological Seminary, who opened their doors for me and aided my search for source material. This is a book that retells many stories that are in other books and I am grateful for all that has been written down and all the translators who made it possible for me to read material written originally in Hebrew. The bibliography that follows is more specific, but I wanted here to express my pleasure in all that I read and learned in the course of working on this book.

I want to thank my agent, Lisa Bankoff, for her friendship and constancy and Claire Wachtel for editing this book with such good, sharp, and thorough care, which turned the final pages into far better ones than had appeared at her desk.

I want to thank my friend Yael Rom for the hours she spent with me in the Israeli Museum and for her support. I want to thank Rabbi Arthur Hertzberg for all he has taught me over the years.

INTRODUCTION

*G*OD BREATHED ON the waters of the world and the story began.

*T*he first tales are about all of us: humankind, our proclivity to evil, our expulsion from Paradise, our pride, our murderous ways. But then in Genesis 11 begins the history of a particular nation that will heed the words of the Lord and follow his ways, seeking goodness and justice at least some of the time. The women in these stories are like the caryatids of Greek architecture. They hold up the structure, they steady the ground, without them there is nothing but broken stones. We see these women riding on camels, feeding their donkeys, carrying wheat on their backs, grinding barley in a stone bowl, picking figs, weaving wool gathered from the sheep and dyed with colors drawn from the fruits of the earth.

We can't forget these women because they belong to us, come with us, across seas in exile. They are the root and we are the newest branches reaching to the sky but attached to the trunk, attached to our story.

There is Sarah in the main east window of the Cathedral of St. Peter at Poitiers. The window was made at the end of the twelfth century. There she is in the Holy Comforter Lutheran Church in Belmont, North Carolina, and in a stained glass panel made in 1485 in the south window of the great Malvern Priory in Worcester, England, and again in a panel of a window behind the altar in Houston's St. Martin's Episcopal church. There her face is framed by gold stars representing the promise of God to multiply her seed. Mosaics, paintings, windows, tell the stories of Rebekah, Rachel, and Leah. Around these women are pages of comment, legends that were written down years later. For Jews, Christians, and Muslims the common story begins here.

Women may not have the central role in the historical record, but these particular women, Sarah, Rebekah, Rachel, and Leah, had great influence on events and stood against the forces of nature and man with enduring courage and suffered no more or less than the men of their time. They too were buffeted by drought and rain, the cruelty of the sword, the lack of power, the tricks of time and nature. Birth and death affected them in ways equal to the men they lived with. Women's choices may have seemed limited, but both genders were bound to circumstances they could hardly control. Men and women together shared the chaos that God left behind when he formed the world out of the abyss.

It does not matter if the words came from a holy source or

were recorded by scribes in various times. It does not matter if God always has the best interest of his people in mind or he sometimes forgets us or grows deaf to our prayers. The words themselves are built now into our understanding of our nature and our place in the universe. This is our treasure.

We name our children Sarah, Rebekah, Rachel, and Leah and in doing so we link them back to the beginning, the camels and the dust and a time when God was visible in human affairs. We use these names because we believe that the story holds a key for us, a key to our own lives. We call our children by these names because these were the names of our grandmothers and great-grandmothers. We link ourselves to those who came before us, and the line is very long. Week after week our fathers have placed their hands on their daughters heads and blessed them, using the names of Sarah, Rebekah, Rachel, and Leah. We have used these names on the prairies of America. We have used them in the fishing towns of New England and where the Quakers sit quietly, and the Methodists gather under their tall white steeples reaching skyward among the evergreens. Little girls go to school with these names in Cleveland, Santa Fe, Buenos Aires, and Paris. These names are used again and again in Israel and in London, Santiago and Pretoria. In the choirs of churches in Mississippi and Los Angeles, Houston and Des Moines, women with these names, black and white, of all denominations are rising to sing their praises to their Lord.

We use these names because we find in them the promise of goodness, strength, and simplicity. We believe that God has heard these names and will bless our children who bear them.

We use these names because they remind us of the sacrifice of women with these names in Nazi Germany, where every Jewish woman had an identity card with the name "Sarah" or "Becky" stamped on it. What was intended as contempt we mark with pride. We use these names because we hope our daughters will endure whatever hardships come their way as did our Matriarchs in their time. These names are not jangling or fashionable. They do not hint of celebrity or stardom. Instead they promise goodness, survival in the face of terrible dangers. They suggest the persistence and beauty and simplicity of the women who have borne these names through the generations.

This book was drawn from a variety of prayer books and texts and Torahs from all major Jewish religious communities. I have used the writing of Rashi and the Rambam, the Zohar, and the collected legends of the Jews. I have used Talmud and midrash and books of interpretation. I have used anthropologists and folklorists and incorporated all into a story of these four women. I have not etched each character in the way that modern fiction demands. I have not given Sarah a stammer and Rachel a limp or a tendency to repeat herself, etc. These are mythic figures, and I have tried not to reduce them to characters such as we might see on our favorite television show or read about in a popular novel. These lives are too awesome for such reduction.

To retell these stories that are so perfectly told and already so heavily embroidered requires a kind of nerve. I dared this in hopes of coming closer to the beginnings of my imaginative world. I did this in hopes that I could take my reader with me into an astonishing time where God's voice could still be heard and we had not yet come so close to destroying creation itself.

Sarah

THE STORY STARTS three thousand years ago in the early 1200s before the Common Era.

The grass blows gently in the wind. The figs ripen. The world is still new, ten generations have lived and died since Noah landed his ark on the ledge of Mount Ararat.

A girl named Sarai sleeps, protected against the night air by her shawl. She will become the mother of a great nation. Through her we will move toward whatever mysterious end awaits. Because of her, God will have a people and a people will have a God.

It was lucky that Sarai was not carried off in infancy by a raging fever, an infection in the ear: lucky that she was not trampled by the mule when she slipped between his feet. Perhaps the bandits that rode past on their way to Egypt stole only the camels and left undisturbed the children hiding in the dark night in the nearby cave. Maybe Sarai became Sarah not because it had always been planned this way but because Sarai had not broken her leg when she tumbled down the gully when she was eight. Only in retrospect does destiny come knocking at the door. In real life it slips in with the germs, with the dust, with the twists of time and geography.

Or perhaps not. It may have been God's intention from the moment He breathed on the deep, to bring Sarai to Abram and Abram to Sarai.

The land in the fertile crescent tolerated the peoples who watched over their sheep, gathered the fruits from the trees, wove cloth from the wool they sheared, and slept on mats in tents made from the hides of their animals. Some lived in small cities, groups banded together to trade. These city dwellers lived behind walls to protect them from the roaming bandits, the fierce despoilers of life and property, the slave hunters, the rapists, the lawless, who were everywhere. The city dwellers built their houses with stones. They had kings to protect them. Today we call them warlords. Then they were commanders of small armies, one hundred men or more. They traded in cloth and grain, in copper and lapis lazuli. And from time to time they invaded one another's camps to steal their camels, to lead away their sheep, to take the gold and silver, to rape the women, to take the children as slaves.

In the late summer they harvested grapes and olives. In the early fall, when the rains began, they planted seeds. Then came two months of cutting flax. Late winter they gathered seeds to eat or press into oil. Then they harvested the barley, and in spring they took the wheat they had sowed.

The wandering clans brought their harvests to the city gates and sold them. They moved with the changing seasons in search of green grass, protection from fierce wind, and always they were looking for water, because without water there was no life. Where the river ran, where the wells were found, there they stayed awhile. There they returned.

Everyone believed in many gods, and these gods were said to inhabit the stone or wood replicas of themselves.

Death was common, men died from small wounds, from a pain in the ear, from a stomachache. Women died in childbirth, the loved wives and the unloved wives all perished when their labor took too long, when the cord was bound around the baby's neck, when they bled into the blankets placed beneath them and no one knew how to stop the bleeding. Children died of small rashes, insect bites, little coughs that grew into rasping calls for breath. They fell into wells or waded too far out in the lake, or were eaten by lions or wandering boars. Little children died of strange fevers, of bowels that would not stop running, of eating the wrong berry from the wrong tree, of scorpion stings.

There were idols that were large and idols that were small and could be stored in a sack or kept by a bedside. There were some idols who may have been offered the blood of newborn children, breaking some mother's hearts that were not made of stone. The idols were offered the choicest part of the calf, the sweetest of delicacies. Scents were burned to please their noses. They were praised and entreated and promised loyalty in return for protection from enemies, and that protection was clearly needed, because terror rode just over the next hill, because famine and drought were not unknown.

We know that the nation of Israel existed by 1207 B.C.E. because a stone tablet, the *mehepthah* stele, was found that listed a number of defeated nations. It said, "Israel is stripped bare wholly lacking in seed."

In the Canaanite land where God in time would send Sarai and her husband, Abram, son of Terah, descendant of Noah, the people once recorded the tale of Baal and Anat. Here is a description of a battle found in the Ugaritic epic cycle:

> Maiden Anat draws near to him
> As is the heart of a cow toward her calf
> As is the heart of a ewe toward her lamb
> So is the heart of Anat for Baal
> She seizes the God Mot
> With sword she cleaves him.
> With fan she winnows him.
> With fire she burns him
> With mill she grinds him
> In fields she sows him
> Birds eat the pieces of him
> Devour the bits of him.

The violence in the human heart was reflected onto the gods.

Robert Graves and Raphael Patai, in their book, *Hebrew Myths*, write that the most powerful idol at the time may have been Aeseroth, a goddess of the womb. Sometimes she was kind and sometimes she was not. Anyone who went out at night and looked up at the moon and the stars and saw the vast expanse of sky that hung over the land understood that mankind was in need of many gods. We were bloodthirsty cruel animals without the teeth and claws of a lion, without the muscles of a panther, lacking the speed of a gazelle, and unless cradled in the arms of more powerful beings, we feared we would not survive.

This was the world that Sarai entered.

*T*he sages say she was thirteen years old when Abram, son of Terah, came to her family and it was agreed that she would marry him. This was in the land of Ur of the Chaldees. The sages say her name meant "princess." The sages also say that she was tall and her face was good to look at.

Sarai may have been the granddaughter of Terah, who is also Abram's father. Terah is a descendant of Noah. She may have been the daughter of Terah's other son Haran and one of his wives. One sage has said so, but he was eager to describe the lineage of the people as starting in one place, in bearing a solid strong root, out of which the great tree of nationhood would spring, one blood, one people. It isn't written in the book of Genesis that Sarai was Terah's granddaughter, but scholars and storytellers have over time added their own interpretations to the bare bones of the tale. In this way the story over the centuries becomes a collective vision of many minds.

*S*arai may have been told of the marriage plan a few weeks before. Would she have hidden her face so the women in the tent would not see the redness in her cheeks? Was she afraid but hopeful, a maiden's hope of the sweet touch of a man?

We do not know that she was better of soul, kinder, or more worthy than her sisters or her neighbors. She was not the only girl whom Terah might have selected for his son, but it is clear that she did not choose Abram. He was her fate. She could not have felt regret or surprise. She must have known since she was a small child that one day a man would come and give her family whatever was demanded in exchange for her, and she would be taken off along with a servant, a donkey, a few blankets. She had no choice, not this man or that, this place to live or that. That is the way it was at that time in all the corners of the known world.

Abram, who was twenty years older than she, has been painted by artists through the years as a fine man with a black beard. Perhaps Sarah watched him dismount from his camel, give the beast to a servant, and order a slave to carry sacks of gold into her uncle's tent.

No one knows the name of Sarai's mother. The mother of the nation cannot have a mother or the story has no beginning. I imagine Sarai's mother has died, perhaps giving birth to Sarai. Such things were not uncommon. Nursemaids, sisters, aunts, would have watched over Sarai. We have no record that Sarah was a child given to dark thoughts or recriminations. We can assume she loved those who would love her and grew strong from whatever nourishment was offered.

Abram must have told Sarai that his God was the only God, the true God, the one power in the universe, and all the other goddesses that she had known were shadows on the wall, pretend beings, false images. Sarai said she understood. His words made her sad. Perhaps Sarai knocked over Aeseroth, the goddess of all things, which had traveled with the family as long as she could remember. Aeseroth could not pick herself up where she had rolled behind a bowl. Perhaps Sarai took a small knife used for cutting wool from sheep and made a long jagged line down the wooden back of the goddess. But a moment later she might have apologized to Aeseroth and given her one of her earrings, a silver loop, which lay in front of the idol now, occasionally catching a ray of light when the tent flap was opened.

Lightning struck one tree but not another. Fate brought death here but not there, no matter how many gods had been offered choice parts, promised devotion, given gifts of golden necklaces. Something beyond all human power sent the wind down into the desert and gave the sheep a good year, planned the swarming of the insects to the flower. The cold came, the great sky could roar, or the ground could blister from heat. Why did the sky not blow away and reveal the place of the gods? Some babies were born dead or without sight or missing a limb. Sometimes the gods protected you and sometimes they mocked. Everything in Sarai's world was uncertain. Now she accepted her husband's words. There was one God and He had His reasons. This knowledge must have brought her comfort.

Maybe she then walked to the river's edge and offered a last prayer to the river goddess. She whispered a hurried farewell to the running water. There was rain in her eyes, and her hands may have hesitated. She may have been cold despite the shawl that she wore. She could hardly see the far rock on the opposite bank of the river where she had played just weeks before with her cousins. And then she went off with Abram to live with his relatives and his slaves and his servant in his encampment nearby.

*T*he Zohar tells us this story about Abram: when God created the world it was unstable and rocked to and fro. God said to the world, "Wherefore rockest thou?" It answered. "I cannot be firm because I have no foundation on which to rest." God thereupon said, "Behold, I intend to raise up in thee a righteous man, Abram, who will love me." Hearing this the world straightaway became firmly established.

No doubt Sarai's life, married to the man that steadied the world, would be exceptional, amazing.

Here is a story from a religious man talking to his disciples centuries later in a small town in Poland: Abram had been traveling alone in a forest and had suddenly come upon a great palace with all the windows lit up and music coming from within, and peacocks walking in the yard, and he saw no one, and when he called no one came to a window. Surely, he said to himself, such a great palace has someone to mind it, to care for the gardens, to watch over it. Then came a terrible voice from the heavens. This is my palace and I am the master. Then the palace disappeared before his eyes. The Hassid is talking about God, a God who spoke to Abram just this way, without palaces but just as forcefully.

There were stories about Abram that were gathered in

books centuries later, but that must have been repeated campfire to campfire, family to family, year after year before anyone thought of writing them down. These stories had been
brought to the women's tents, by travelers selling trinkets,
camel herders looking for blankets, slaves talking under the
stars.

These are the tales that Sarai may have heard about the man
who would become her husband. These are the tales I read in
slightly different versions in Louis Ginzberg's *Legends of the
Jews,* as well as in many of the footnotes in translations of Genesis. Did they amaze Sarai, these stories, or were they alarm-
ing? Would she have preferred a less remarkable husband?
Like Sarai, we all fall into our lives and then we live them.

The night Abram was conceived a comet appeared and devoured the stars in the four quadrants of the sky until only the
light of the comet's tail illuminated the darkness. King Nimrod's hastily assembled astrologers told him that soon a male
child would be born who would prove that there was a greater
king than he, greater than all the gods together. The king ordered that all pregnant women be gathered into one fortress
and be guarded by the king's own men, and midwives would
deliver the women. At the time of birth the midwives were ordered under penalty of death to smother all male infants as
they took their first suckle at their mothers' breasts. The females would be allowed to live and their mothers given silver
and gold. Seventy thousand male babies were murdered in that
House of Pregnant Women.

🌿

This legend that has been passed down through the centuries, elder to younger, elder to younger, until finally written down and gathered by the keepers of stories.

Terah was an idol maker in Nimrod's kingdom. He was a man who would never defy the king, so when he suspected his wife, Emaltali, might be pregnant, he prepared to send her off into the king's custody. Emaltali denied she was pregnant to her husband. He put his hands on her belly to feel for himself, and miraculously the fetus rose up into her chest, hiding from his father's probing fingers. As her time came close, she ran away from her husband's house, away from all friends and neighbors who might be tempted to betray her, and all alone in the usual pain and blood and fear, she delivered her son in a dark cave high above a running river. After a day she left the cave, afraid that Terah would come after her and kill the child. First she cradled the baby in her arms, she sang him a lullaby. She said to him, "It is better that you should perish here in this cave than that my eye should behold you dead at my breast." Later a sage wrote, "She said, 'May the Lord be with you, not fail you, nor forsake you.'" Maybe she said that. She wrapped him in her shawl and turned her back. Strange as this story is, much later, a generation later, a slave girl named Hagar in the desert will place her son at a distance so she too will not have to see him die.

It was said that the Angel Gabriel then came down from the heavens above and placed his little finger in the infant's mouth, and from his finger flowed milk and nourishment, and a warm breeze blew and the child laughed his first laugh. Think of the ceiling of the Sistine Chapel. There God gives Adam life through the touch of a finger, another version perhaps of this story. There were in those days many goddesses who would easily be expected to nurse an abandoned infant, but in the tale that has come to us, the milk is from a finger of a male: why not? The world for better or worse was drifting away from its goddesses and turning toward a male god.

The story goes on to say that within ten days this amazing child could walk and talk and left the cave. His mother came back, hoping against hope that some animal had come along to suckle him, that a miracle had been granted her. She found Abram striding along the riverbank. He told her that he had been left by his mother in a cave. She embraced him, told him she was his mother, and wept with joy.

Could Sarai have heard this story. Could she have believed it?

It would have been hard to decide which tale was more improbable, that one or the next.

Sages told that Abram as a young boy had looked up at the moon and thought it was God, and in the morning he saw that his God had been devoured by the sun, so he thought that perhaps the sun was God. Then he saw that the sun sank down and the stars came out. He thought that the stars were each gods that controlled the world, but they too disappeared with dawn. Puzzling over this, he decided that only one God could make all this happen. "There was," he announced to his disapproving father whose living after all came from chiseling idols from the finest of woods found in the forest, "only one God." His father was angry and punished him severely.

His father went on selling idols. Abram began to talk all over the town about his discovery. There was only one God, who made the world, one God, not an idol, but an invisible power, whose hand stretched over all creation, a true authority, the only God that deserved to be praised. Did anyone believe him? The storytellers do not say.

Another story told about Abram tells of how he went through town, selling the wooden idols his father had made in his shop. But Abram believed in one God, who was invisible, like the air, His hands cradling the entire world from Dan to Beersheba. He had breathed life into all creation, making the sun and the moon, the smallest of snails, the wildest of beasts, the forest, the lakes, the wide sweep of desert, the limbs and heart of man and woman. One day Abram was left alone in his father's workshop. He took an ax and smashed all the idols into splinters of wood. He left one large idol standing and in its hand he put the ax. Terah came back and saw his hard work destroyed; noses, hands, and feet of his creatures were strewn across the floor. Terah said to his son, "How dare you do this." "I didn't do it, Father," said Abram. "It was the large idol, see the ax is in his hand." Terah wept with rage. "Don't lie," he said to his son. "The idol is only wood. I made him with my own hands. He has no power. He cannot move. You are the one who did this." "You are right," said Abram. "The idol cannot move itself any more than a dead branch of a tree can bring itself to the fire or protect itself from the ax. The one true God deserves our prayers and our praise." I found this story in the notes of several prayer books.

Terah went on making and selling idols because that is how

he earned his keep. Abram talked to all he met on the road, in the marketplace, in the caravans that passed by the town, telling them about the one true God. But King Nimrod remembered the words of his astrologers, and when word came to him about Abram's strange teachings he ordered Terah to bring his son to the palace. Abram went with his father and his brother Haran. Abram stood before the king, who said to Abram, "I am a god. Tell all my court that I am the king of all the world, there is no king more powerful than I."

Abram refused. He said, "Only Eloheim, the One God above, is my God. I bow to no other." King Nimrod was both afraid and angry. He ordered a large furnace to be brought to the square at the base of the palace steps. He ordered wood to be piled up in the furnace and a fire lit. He ordered his men to throw Abram into the fire right there in front of the assembled people so all could see that the true power belonged to Nimrod not to this God of Abram. Two of the king's men grabbed Abram by the arms and pulled him close to the blazing fire. At once the flames leapt out of the furnace and turned the soldiers' skin to black charcoal. Screaming in pain, they died. King Nimrod was shaking and his face was pale as a morning moon, but he ordered two more of his men to drag Abram toward the furnace. They too met the same fate, with the flames like long tongues consuming them, so they released Abram, who remained untouched by fire. The king's advisors gathered around him.

The Evil Impulse, Satan, disguised as an astrologer, suggested to the king that they build a catapult and from a safe distance hurl Abram into the flames. It took hours to build the contraption but at last it was ready. Perhaps Terah wept. His son looked so strong, stood so tall, had such a fine face with eyes that reflected no fear, no interest in the hammering and sawing and lifting of beams that went on around him, as the king's carpenters constructed the machine that would bring his death. After being placed by the king's soldiers into the catapult, he was thrown forward into the mouth of the fiery furnace. He stood there a moment inside the fire while all the people gasped. Some of the women covered their eyes. The flames immediately died down, and in between the logs, the people could see violets growing and yellow daisies clustered. Abram stepped out of the furnace unhurt.

Haran, Abram's brother, saw that the fire had not burned Abram and he wanted the crowd to admire him. When he stepped into the furnace, suddenly the flames burst forth again, just where he was standing, and he sank to his knees and died. Terah cried out in grief. Abram bowed to the ground with the sorrow of losing his brother. Later a sage would write, "Haran did not believe in the One God of Abraham. He only wanted his brother's glory and so he died." The rabbis believed that intentions matter as much as deeds. A pure heart is necessary if God is to be pleased.

This is the terrible fire used by those in power to enforce their authority. It is the fire that burnt Rabbi Meir when he refused to honor the Roman emperor. His torturers wrapped him in wet wool so that his death would be prolonged. It is the fire of the Inquisition in Spain. It is the fire that ripped the bodies of saints and martyrs.

This is also the fire of the burnt offering to God. This burnt offering is an appeasement for our sins, an apology for our failures, and a wild hope that God will accept a charred animal in place of our lives, which can never evade the shadow of death. This is also the fire that renews our forests, that keeps the cold from our bones, that allows us to nourish ourselves. It is the fire of the candle that shines on the family table. The angels had been created out of fire before Adam took his first breath, so say the sages. It is not fire that harms us but the way we turn it against our fellow creatures.

Noah survived the flood. Abram survived the fire, according to this story.

The king feared Abram's God. He told Abram to leave the city and he did, with his father and his father's household. Out of fear of Abram's God the sages say the king gave them riches. They went into the hills, and goats and sheep, camels and cows became their companions. They set up tents and followed the pastures from place to place. They prospered.

These tales about Abram are important in Sarai's story because they tell us of the sacred nature of the task ahead. Sarai is now wrapped in the miraculous, the holy, the unusual. In most respects her days will apparently pass as those of all other women around her, and yet she is, as Abram's wife, linked to God and to our future. These stories are fantastic, jagged, irrational. This is not the way we tell stories to one another today. Pharaohs' wicked plan to kill the firstborn male is echoed in Nimrod's orders to kill in the House of Pregnant Women. Abram's mother is not the last woman to rescue her baby from the edict of a wicked king. We think of Moses floating in his basket in the bulrushes. This story shows us a father, Terah, who will sacrifice his son for his god even if that god is merely his king. The sacrifice of sons is a rope that links together many stories hundreds of years apart.

The hero of these legends appears to be Abram, but Abram is not Abram without Sarai. He has the main speaking part, that is true. He is the first to recognize the one God indivisible. But his wife is his helpmeet, his soul mate. She stands with him so that he does not have to bear alone the immense efforts every human must make since Adam and Eve were forced from the Garden. Together they work to feed themselves, to take pride in their days, to look forward without fear. Sarai is the one who keeps him from the terrible aloneness of human life, who diverts him from its shortness, its brutality.

Before a half year had passed she was no longer Sarai but a part of something called Sarai-Abram, a coupling. They could not follow each other into their dreams, but when they woke, the other was there, arms ready to fold around the other. Abram said God had blessed him. She felt blessed too.

It says in the Stone Edition of Genesis that Abraham always honored his wife by pitching her tent before his own.

But I imagine that as the months passed and she bled again and again, she became sad. Her old nurse comforted her. The womenfolk encouraged her with stories of other women who had to wait a long time before they brought forth a child. Sarai hoped. She prayed to the one true God that Abram had taught her would hear her prayers. He did not. Did Abram think this was a test? Again and again he must have promised Sarai that a child would come. But despite his confidence, despite his joy in his beautiful wife, despite his own entreaties to the Holy One, Sarai did not conceive. Was this a curse cast by a witch, a goddess that Abram had forsaken, who demanded her part of the first fruits of the harvest? A sage reports that the neighbors said it was just such a curse. Some thought Abram had cast dirt in the faces of the only gods in the world and they would take revenge on him so he would crawl back to them begging to be forgiven. Sarai did not believe these whispers. Sarai and Abram held fast to their belief in the one true God. Sarai must have been certain that God did not hate Abram.

She was right.

Custom allowed Abram to divorce his barren wife, Sarai, and send her back to her family. He did not. Centuries later Rabbi Eliezer said, "Whoever divorces his first wife even the altar sheds tears because of him."

The land they lived in was not ruled by one king. It was claimed by several, all of whom wanted tithes of grain, calves from the herd, sheep from the fold, all of whom sent men with swords to roam the countryside. Abram slept with his own sword by his side, and often he would rise suddenly at a strange sound, a jackal's howl, a fox crawling toward the sheep, or the hoofbeats of camels approaching.

The years went on. Sarai changed from a young girl to a woman.

She worked alongside her servants, roasting the meat, grinding the grain, picking the olives, thrashing the grapes, and filling the jars with oil. She beat the sand out of the blankets and washed the clothes in the water, and when there was little water she poured with care, she went without. She watched the sky for signs of rain.

We do not have reports of her saying extraordinary words, discovering new methods of planting, exploring the unexplored. We do not see her special devotion to God. What we can easily imagine is the daily life of a woman whose hands lifted and lowered, whose fingers wove and spun and stirred and held. She was a woman of valor whose acts of bravery consisted of small deeds of endurance. We see her walking, carrying a basket of barley. We see her unwinding her head scarf for the night. Her long hair lying loose on her shoulders. We see her living day after day under the approving eye of God.

One morning just as the dawn touched the horizon of the desert, Sarai woke and walked out into the new morning. She must have seen her husband running toward her. He grabbed her arm and pulled her inside. Perhaps he had heard a calf crying in pain and had risen and dressed and gone out to find it. He looked around and saw nothing but the now pale sky, the quickly fading star that hung low above. Genesis tells us that a voice came to him and it was God and God told him to leave his land and his father's house and go to a distant land. God had said that He would make of Abram a great nation and He had said I will bless you and you shall be a blessing. Sarai must have known that Abram could only become a great nation if he had a child, and now God had promised him a child and so God had promised her a child. Sarai did not hesitate. It says in the Zohar, the thirteenth-century book of mystical writings, that a man is forbidden to take his wife to a foreign land without her consent. This must have been an old tradition among the tribes. In this journey Sarai would have had a choice. She agreed.

A sage, referring perhaps to the confusion at the Tower of Babel and the Flood and the banishment of Cain, said when God told Abraham to set forth, this was the first time since the expulsion from Eden that God promised blessings instead of bringing curses down on the heads of his feckless creation. This is a turning point, when man and God must have first felt for each other something like love.

Sarai had agreed to leave all that was familiar to her. She would journey to a place that as yet had no name, that might be full of beasts waiting to tear a traveler apart. It might be full of wild men and armies that would kill or rape or enslave her. It might be a place without flowers or trees or water. If so, she could die from thirst or hunger. Would she have had more confidence in this journey if God had spoken directly to her? Of course she would. But she had to take satisfaction in the fact that of all the men on earth, the Lord God had selected her husband for a special task, a long journey, and he had agreed. She already knew that her husband, a man God talked to (not a man like so many others who talked to gods and heard nothing in return), was good of heart, pure in his soul, kind to those who worked for him, careful of the needs of his father, and faithful to his kin, a man who was strong of arm but stronger still in his love for all creation.

I imagine that Sarai herself was not so sure of her own goodness, her own love for all around, but she would try, try to be like her husband, a person of decency in a place where invaders could come and mutilate little children, where your grain belonged to you only as long as you could protect it, where every night snakes or scorpions could enter your tent and take your life, or a camel could stumble and smash your bones. I believe that Sarai followed Abram without question or reproach.

The sages tell us that when a woman marries she should cleave to her husband, but the fact that they have written down these words reveals that this needed to be said, that "cleaving" is never as easy as it sounds. It is hard to go away, to leave behind the known, the place where you are known. It is hard to venture out, even with a mate at your side. The bravery of all the women who have done this cleaving is amazing if often unheralded.

Abram was seventy-five at this time. That is what it says in Genesis. How we read and understand these numbers is not so simple. We should not think of a seventy-five-year-old man who today might be retired from his life's work, or a seventy-five-year-old man who may have had a stroke, or one who is still working—perhaps on a book—but whose hair is white, whose limbs are not steady, whose back may curve, whose hand trembles. The seventy-five that describes Abram at this moment finds him in the middle of his life, filled with strength and purpose and virility.

Remember at the time of this tale we are closer to creation itself and man was given at first a longer span of years. Maybe it took a millennia or two for Adam's and Eve's immortality to wear off. Maybe we just imagine our ancestors living longer than we do because they seem so much greater, so much more important than we are. Maybe someone just couldn't count.

Think of Sarai, still young, vibrant, beautiful as she set out from Haran, leaving Terah's place with livestock, a hand-maiden or two, some men who had been purchased in Haran, slaves who might one day be freed, who were needed to help with the small herd, a few women to care for the washing and the fetching of water, all their worldly goods on the backs of a few donkeys. A camel, perhaps two or three plodding behind, with the tent materials, rugs, and small chests of household things, roped onto their saddles. They took with them Lot, who was Abram's nephew and Sarai's cousin. He was family; his father, Haran, was gone. He belonged then to Abram's family.

Without Lot our history would not be the same, so it was a very good thing that he was not left behind. The sages do not speak with much affection about Lot. He was a man that trouble would find, but the Lord had a plan and our sages knew that it was no use to whisper reproaches into the musty pages before them. Lot was part of the story, his line would lead to kings. He might have been a bent branch, but he was a branch nevertheless on the great tree that would become the Story, the Truth, the Way It Was. He was part of the begats and so could not be left behind.

I imagine Sarai had not given up hope that she would be granted the normal way for women, that she would hold an infant in her arms and let it suckle the ample milk that would flow from her own breasts. Perhaps she dreamed each month that this had happened. Surely she felt certain several times when her blood came late, two days, three days, but always before the sixth day the blood began to flow. No doubt she would hide her disappointment from the female slave in the tent and say nothing to Abram, who must have hidden his own disappointment from her.

But now Sarai might have thought as she mounted the donkey that the new land with its new air might affect her body, the new land might bring new possibilities, perhaps it was there, in the place where God had told Abram he would show him, perhaps there she would become pregnant.

Solomon Ben Isaac, the famous Rashi, the eleventh-century commentator from Troyes, France, said, "For whoever is childless is accounted as dead." Some sages went even further and said, "It would be better to be dead than not to have a child." The survival of the group depended on the fertility of its members. There were no effective medicines, so few second chances. If one fell ill or broke a bone or ate a poisonous fruit, death waited. The birth of children was essential for the survival of the community. No wonder it loomed so large in these our first stories. But even without this pressure to survive most of us still wish to bear life, to hold a child of our own in our arms. The centuries have not replaced that need with another.

The journey to the land of Canaan was long. How many days exactly no one knows. Perhaps even Abram and Sarai lost count. They surely stopped here and there to let the animals rest. I imagine that they stopped because of a heavy rain that flooded the river they were about to cross. They may have waited the better part of the month before the waters subsided. It's possible that they took a week to sit by the mound of dirt that covered the burial site of a young slave who had died of a head wound he suffered when a limb of a tree fell on him as they were passing through a forest.

At last, however, they crossed into Canaan. The land was green and the soil was rich. Everywhere they stopped they had to find water. Without water the animals would die. The rocks, the distant mountains, the hills and valleys, were all new to them. The air smelled of the far sea and the pines. It was different from the air they were used to. The constellations had changed places in the sky. Each day they gathered wood for the fires. They crossed long distances slowly but with determination. Abram and Sarai and those who came with them continued to Sechem. There they found the Terebinth (a grove of oak trees) of Moreh. On their way they could have seen the tents of the Canaanites that were pitched by the rivers, clung to the green hills. They might have also seen the tents of the Amorites, the Kenits and the Kadomites, and the Kenizzites, who were invaders from the Syrian desert. They may have passed at night, moving silently as possible behind the tents of Perizzites, the Hittites, the Jebusites. The land that the Lord had brought them to was not empty, not waiting for them to arrive, but already home to others who had their claims, who had their wells, who would regard the strangers as intruders. Even then it was like that.

I imagine that Sarai was standing at the edge of a marsh when Abram came toward her. His face was radiant. In Genesis it says that God had visited him and had spoken to him. "To your seed I will give this land."

Then Abram built an altar there to the Lord who had appeared to him, to thank him for his words, to signal to all the passing Canaanites that a believer in the one true God had passed through here. He decided to go to the high country east of Bethel, and after several days' travel he pitched his tent with Bethel to the west and Ai to the east and he built there another altar to the Lord, and he told Sarai to be grateful to the Lord for all the wonders of creation.

Sarai must have been grateful, but perhaps she had certain reservations. Her monthly bleeding was uninterrupted. All of the servants and the slaves and the men who had followed Abram to the land of Canaan knew that she had not conceived, and she was ashamed. Perhaps she wondered why the Lord, who loved Abram so much that he came to him and talked to him, did not love her also, and bless her with a child. Perhaps her affection for the Lord was less than perfect, but she did have something to reproach him for and no doubt she was often sad.

One of the sages, wishing to honor Sarai, said, "Among the seven female prophets, Sarah is the one with the closest, most direct relationship with God." Nevertheless she was barren.

*I*n the land of the Canaanites bears roamed the high forests and sometimes came down to the plains to steal a calf, to fish in the streams. There were lions moving about among the evergreens and oaks. There were monkeys and panthers and wild onagers. Abram and Sarai tended their flock, and it increased. They gathered fruits from the trees, nuts and olives and pounded them with stones. They had oil for cooking and the hides of the animals to keep them warm. They traded with the tribes around them.

But then the rains did not come and the ground dried and the topsoil blew away in the wind. Then the grass turned brown and the sheep nibbled at fields of dried grass and lifeless weed. For many months the carrion birds circled the camp. Abram and his men dug deep into the earth, hoping to find a pool of buried water, an underground stream that they could channel into a well. Piles of dusty soil could be seen across the valley. But no water was found.

It was not just the lack of rain that had devastated the land but also the ravages of the warring tribes, which had taken their toll on the seedlings and on the grass. Acres and acres had been burned as each warrior tried to ruin the grazing grounds of his enemy. Fires were set to granaries, the great holes in the ground where soy and beans were stored were burnt and their contents destroyed.

*G*enesis 12:10 says, "There was famine in the land and Abram went down to Egypt to sojourn there, for the famine was grave in the land."

Abram saw that everywhere he went the trees were shrunk and withered. Brown was the color even of the water, which had dried in the riverbeds. Abram and Sarai needed to move to a place where seeds could sprout. If they did not they might die. Once more they rolled their rugs, filled their chests with necessities of life—the cooking pots, the bedding. The tents were folded and placed across the backs of the donkeys, who brayed and howled, hungry as they were. They were passed by caravans of others who had reached the end of their patience and were now moving down to Egypt. This bountiful land, the beautiful land, the land of milk and honey sometimes was not. Was this because of sin in the human heart? Was this because God was displeased with his creation, or were long dry seasons a necessary part of a divine plan?

Rashi said that "famine came to test Abram, to see if he had qualms about God's promises."

As they came close to Egypt, which was just over the next hill, they passed a shallow lake, and the camels and the donkeys and the dog drank and Abram's household filled their vessels with water. It was not clean water but it was wet. Just yards offshore a herd of water buffalo standing knee-deep bellowed into the air. But it was water, and Abram thanked God for providing it on their journey.

The sages tell the story this way. Abram knelt down to the water's edge to drink. His mouth was dry and his throat was sore from the days of breathing dust. Sarai knelt by his side and cupped her hands to fill them with water. The sun behind them glistened on the water and suddenly Abram saw Sarai's reflection. She was beautiful. Abram realized at that moment that she was too beautiful.

When most people think of the Matriarch they think of an old woman whose waist is wide, with hair on her lip and crevices in her face. Whatever power she may have comes from age and experience. They forget that even dried-up and withered women were once young—and Sarai was a woman who caught and held the eye of all who saw her. Abram said to Sarai, "When the Egyptians see you and say 'She is his wife,' they will kill me while you they will let live. Say please that you are my sister, so that it will go well with me on your count and I shall stay alive because of you." Abram distrusted the Egyptians and believed they were sexually immoral. This, a sage says, was because it was known that the Egyptians had descended from Ham, and Ham had taken more of the land than was given to him by Noah. Ham it was said was a man who would steal women and rape girls. Of course each small nation distrusted the other, each tribe thought the other was evil, and for this we need no tainted ancestors who survived the great Flood.

Sarai must have considered his words. It was true that Abram might be killed because someone would desire her. It was also true that something unspeakable might happen to her if she appeared to have no husband, to be a woman available to other men. What did Sarai think then? There is no record. Certainly she did not shout or wail. But perhaps there was a hush inside her head, a silence that was terrible where her unspoken words, her barely thought words, waited. Abram must have trusted that God would protect her. Sarai may have been less sure. Perhaps she was surprised that Abram valued his own life above hers.

*T*here is another story from the sages that we find in the *Legends of the Jews* by Louis Ginzberg. A man of Abram's virtue would at least try to protect his wife and not simply offer her to the border guards. In order to protect Abram from charges of cowardice, this story was told. The Redak says that Abram, in telling Sarai to pretend to be his sister, chose the lesser of two evils. It is hard to believe that the man whom God chose to begin his favored nation had a cold heart, and the Redak defends him against the unspoken charge.

The story was told by Robert Graves and Raphael Patai in *Hebrew Myths* that Abram placed Sarai inside a chest, and small holes were bored in the top so she could breathe. They approached the border. They unloaded their goods before the guards. "What have you in this chest?" said one, poking with his sword at the lid. "I have beans," he said, "pounds of beans to feed my people." The guards tipped the chest on its side. "This is not heavy enough for beans," said one. "What have you there?" "I have a rug that had belonged to my father, that I didn't want spoiled by water on our journey." The guards picked up the chest. "There is no rug in here. What are you bringing into Egypt?" Abram tried once more. "I am bringing a few bars of gold and silver and I will give them to you when I am on the other side. What use is gold and silver to me if we have no food to eat and the animals sicken and die." The guards laughed. The pharaoh would have them killed if they took bribes, and Pharaoh had spies everywhere. They took the chest into a tent and pried open the lid.

Rabbi Judah said that when the lid was opened, a light like the sun shone forth, blinding the guards. The light was Sarai's virtue and her beauty. Sarai lay there on her back, her hands folded across her chest. "How beautiful she is," said one guard. "More beautiful than any woman I have ever seen." "Who is she?" the guard asked Abram, pushing him down to the ground. "She is my sister," said Abram. The guards pulled Sarai out of the chest. "Is this true?" one asked. "It is true," said Sarai. "Our father and mother are the same." Her eyes must have burned with the tears she did not dare release. She would not have looked at Abram. Perhaps she would have preferred to have been turned to dust in the drought and the famine of the Canaanite hills rather than to dishonor herself, to be so dishonored in Egypt. Perhaps she was ashamed of her tempting body and tried to cover her face with her hands. She kept her head down. With her eyes she stared at the boots of the guards. She would not look at Abram. She must have feared for her virtue and her life.

I believe her heart split and was perhaps never again as strong as it had been.

*I*s it mere coincidence that a woman is also placed inside of a chest and smuggled across a border in the opening tale of the *Arabian Nights*? Stories repeat themselves, change details, while creating echos that seem to bounce through the centuries from one landscape to another. When the Greeks lost Helen to Paris a twenty-year war followed. God brings Sarai back to her rightful husband in a far shorter and less bloody tale.

*T*he story goes on. The guards were now in a very good mood. One opened a flask of local wine. Here, they offered

Abram, a drink. One of the guards put his hand on Sarai's shoulder and pulled her toward him. She let out a small cry, like that of a lamb taken from its mother. "Stop," said one of the other guards. "The pharaoh's courtiers must see her. They will reward us for the gift." Sarai turned to Abram, but he did nothing, stood still as a statue. I imagine that Sarai was tempted for the first time since leaving her father's house to pray to the goddess Aeseroth for help. A female would understand, she might have thought. But then the words did not come. "Trust in God," Abram had said.

Hyrcanus, a prince of Pharaoh's household, was called. It took a while for the messenger to reach the palace and for the prince to return to the border.

During the wait, Sarai would accept no drink or offer of bread. She would not look at her captors. Hyrcanus arrived, and when he saw Sarai he clapped his hands in pleasure. Pharaoh would reward him for bringing this beautiful woman into the palace. Immediately he gave Abram pearls and the ruby ring that was on his own finger. Abram took the jewels. Perhaps, although the sages didn't record it, he tried to put the ring on Sarai's finger, but she made a fist with both hands as he approached. The guards led her off to a waiting wagon where a team of donkeys would bring her to the palace gates.

Sarai may have thought to herself that if she had borne Abram a child he would not have let her go so easily. Was she no longer of value to him?

I imagine that Sarai turned toward Abram, standing with the pharaoh's soldiers beside the mahogany chest, and stared at him as if seeing him for the first time. She may have seen him loading into the chest bars of gold and vases of silver that had been offered by Hyrcanus. She saw handfuls of diamonds and strings of pearls on velvet cushions. Seeing this wealth placed carefully in Abram's chest could not have pleased Sarai. His good fortune was not necessarily hers.

No longer would Sarai have assumed that Abram shared her destiny, that his God was hers, that he would sacrifice his life for her. It would have seemed more likely that she had been asked to sacrifice everything for him. He would not later want a wife he had sold to another man. She would not be able to return to him. She would have to remain forever among strangers, a woman now enslaved, a concubine not a wife.

She may have prayed to God to save her from Pharaoh. "I am in your hands, O Lord, I am under your wings, O Lord." She could have repeated the words again and again. But why should God rescue her, the Holy One Blessed Be He, when her own husband so easily called her his sister, and allowed her to be removed from his side? How would God measure her worth when her husband valued her so little? Or maybe she was not as troubled as I imagine. Perhaps her trust in both Abram and the Lord was so great that she had little fear of the outcome. The sages do not tell us what she felt. That was not their concern.

After Pharaoh had handed Sarai over to his women slaves to prepare her for the evening, it says in Genesis 12:16, "And it went well with Abram on her count, and he had sheep, and cattle and donkeys, and male and female slaves that he had insisted on giving Abram gifts of many sheep and oxen and she-asses and male and female slaves, and she-asses and camels."

The story goes on: Sarai now waits in the pharaoh's chamber for her new master to arrive. If Sarai is taken by the pharaoh she will no longer be fit to be the mother of the people, Abram's wife. It doesn't matter that it will not be her choice. The fact of the sexual act would in those times, in many times, have marked her as a fallen women who would have been ostracized or worse by her own kind.

Pharaoh was eager for his prize.

In the Apocryphon, among the Dead Sea Scrolls, there is a song that Hyrcanus sang at the feast that night before the pharaoh went to the chamber where Sarai waited:

> *"How beautiful is Sarai*
> *Her long fine glossy hair,*
> *Her shining eyes, her charming nose,*
> *The radiance of her face*
> *How full her breasts, How white*
> *Her skin*
> *Her arms how goodly, how delicate*
> *Her hands*
> *Their soft palms and long slender fingers*
> *How lissome her legs, How plump her thighs*
> *Of all the virgins that beneath the canopy walk*
> *None can compare with Sarai*
> *The fairest women underneath the sky*
> *Excellent in her beauty*

Yet with all that she is sage
And prudent and gracefully moves her hands."

*B*ut not all of the commentators, the long line of rabbis and scholars that examined every word of this story, found Sarai's beauty worthy of such praise. One of them said, "Sarah is to Eve as a monkey is to man." Maybe this one was a sour soul not so fond of women or a man with a wretched wife who tormented him night and day, or perhaps he had meant that as the years take us further and further away from Paradise increasingly our animal nature emerges. It wasn't necessary to insult Sarah in order to compliment Eve.

The sages also dared to offer criticism of the moral choices of both Sarai and Abram. Moses Maimonides, known as the Rambam, writing in the twelfth century said, "Know that our father Abraham inadvertently committed a great sin by placing his virtuous wife in a compromising situation because of his fear of being killed. He should have trusted in God to save him."

I imagine after a feast Abram lay down on a soft feather bed in a room with red silk curtains on the walls and a golden dish by the bed filled with water for drinking.

Sarai was dressed now by the pharaoh's slaves in a robe of silver and a shawl with golden threads and her eyes were painted with kohl in the manner of Egyptian women. She sat on the bed shivering in fear. I assume Abram longed to go to her but knew he would be killed if he did so. He was ashamed of his lie. He was ashamed of himself, but he trusted in the Lord, who had spoken to him and made promises to him. He trusted that his wife, who would be the mother of a great nation, would not be sullied now, here at the border of Egypt. He waited.

This is the story that was told generation to generation and can be found in several collections of Jewish legends.

Then God sent down an angel. The angel was not visible to Pharaoh, but Sarai could see him in the room, the wide spread of his wings, the dark curls that hung down his back, the hugeness of him, his arms thick as the trunk of an oak tree. (*Angel* is an archaic Greek word meaning "chief.") This Angel Gabriel held in his hands a long stick. As Pharaoh approached the bed he took off his clothes and left them in a pile on the floor for his slave to gather in the morning. What a good night, he intended to have, what a delicious prospect the beautiful woman on the bed offered him! He leaned over Sarai. "Stop trembling," he might have said. "I order you to stop that trembling." She lay still. He put his hand on her sandal strap, but before he could remove it, the angel who was standing behind him hit him with his stick. Pharaoh cried out in pain, "What was that?" He stood up. He saw nothing. He reached forward for Sarai's dress, intending to pull it up over her knees. The angel came forward again and hit him hard, harder than Pharaoh had ever been hit before. "Who dares to attack me?" he roared in anger and whirled around to face his attacker. But he saw no one. Sarai said nothing, but she was glad. Her prayers had been answered. Sarai whispered to the angel, telling him when to strike Pharaoh. "Now," she said as he reached for her breast. "Wait," she said as Pharaoh sat rocking at her side, recovering from the blow.

Another version of the same story was repeated by Rashi.

Suddenly Pharaoh grabbed his genitals. Sores had appeared on his organ, running puss-filled sores. He wept with pain. He reached for Sarai's hand, and the angel hit him between his shoulder blades. There were red sores now in all his private places. His organ was aching, the sores were running. Pharaoh looked at the walls of his bedroom. He saw leprosy on the curtains, leprosy on the bedstead, on the beams and pillars of his chamber. His eunuchs, who had waited outside the door, entered when he cried out. Their faces too were covered with leprosy or perhaps ringworm, scald head, and vitiligo, and their genitals were oozing with pus. A slamming of doors was heard throughout the palace, chairs fell over, vases were smashed, a wind came up out of the desert, and it was a pestilential wind.

The wives of Pharaoh cried out in fever, his children woke with sweat on their foreheads, rashes appeared on all their limbs, some were choking, others were clasping their stomachs in pain. A great cry of horror went through the palace, a call for medicine, mercy, water, came from every room, except Abram's. The wind blew gently there, and the curtains lifted in the breeze as though all were normal.

"What has happened?" Pharaoh said to Sarai. She sat up in the bed. "My Lord, the one true God who is not made of wood or stone but stands above the world and holds us all in his regard has sent this plague down on you. Do not touch me," she said. Now the pharaoh stood as far away from Sarai as he could without leaving the room. "Who are you?" he asked. Sarai was silent. "Answer me," he called out. He was a ruler accustomed to obedience. The pharaoh took a step forward toward her, but the angel hit him hard right behind his knees. "Who are you?" he asked now in a small voice, almost a child's voice. "I am the wife of the man you thought was my brother," said Sarai. "My Lord has protected me." Dawn was now approaching. Pharaoh woke up his entire household. "Bring me the man from Canaan," he shouted.

Abram was brought before the pharaoh. He saw immediately that Sarai had not been harmed. Her face was more beautiful than ever. Perhaps she looked at him not like an adoring girl but like a woman who understands everything. She had not yet forgiven him. "I am Sarai's husband," Abram said. "If you harm me my God will do far worse to you and all those in your kingdom than he has done through the night."

Pharaoh said, "Why did you not tell me she was your wife? Why did you say, 'She is my sister' so that I took her to me as wife? Now here is your wife. Take her and get out!" Pharaoh told his soldiers to take Abram and Sarai and all that he had given him and lead them to the border, where they would stay unharmed till the famine in the land of Canaan had ended.

As soon as the pharaoh had given this command his sores began to heal. The bruises on his back and his legs faded away as if they had never been there. "Your God is powerful," said the pharaoh to Abram. The sages tell us that he decided to give his own daughter to Sarai, one that had been born to one of his concubines. She would be Sarai's own handmaiden. According to the sages her name was Hagar, and she was very young and strong.

Rashi tells us that the pharoah, observing the miracles that God did for Abram, said to his daughter as she was led away to join Abram's household, "It is better to be a handmaiden in Abram's household than a princess in mine." Sarai was surely glad of the gift, although likely filled with dislike of the girl's father, who had so frightened her. She must have wondered about Abram. Who after all was he? Had God approved of his choice to have her call him brother?

This story is told by Louis Ginzberg in his book *Legends of the Jews* and it is referred to and repeated in parts in the footnotes of prayer books that line the pews in small and large, orthodox and less orthodox, synagogues. Because Pharaoh had not harmed Sarai and had allowed Abram to keep all the treasure he had been given, Abram sent a messenger to the palace telling the pharaoh to come to his tents as soon as possible and he would give him a precious gift in return. The pharaoh was afraid to go and afraid not to go. He went with half his army just in case this was a trick. When he arrived Abram served him a meal made from a spring lamb and accompanied with good wine and spread a rug down on the ground for the two men to sit. After the meal Abram taught Pharaoh and his courtiers the astronomy and mathematics that he had learned as a boy from the Chaldeans.

Several sages noted that the suffering of the nation in the centuries that followed was caused by Abram's all too willing sacrifice of his wife's virtue in order to save his own life. It may be as many believe that God keeps track of a person's good deeds and rewards them in time, in His own way, sometimes in a manner that man, with his limited vision, cannot understand. In which case He may also punish man for his mistakes, causing future generations to suffer because of the sins of their forefathers. But it seems unlikely that God would punish so many of the seed of Abraham for an act that, selfish as it was, did end well, assuring his survival as well as increasing his wealth and power.

It's a puzzle. Perhaps Abram knew all along that God would protect Sarai better than he himself would be able to do. But search as we may, we cannot find any words to support that idea. Is guilt inherited? Is punishment spun out through the generations? Are we single souls capable of moral choice, or are we simply parts of the whole like bees in a hive, like cells in a body?

Sarai must have been thankful that she had been spared the pharaoh's hands, his coarse wishes so firmly denied. She must also have appreciated that the angel of the Lord had allowed her to determine when and where the stick would fall on the lustful, foul pharaoh's body. She must have forgiven Abram. Many centuries ago a sage wrote, "It is better to dwell in a desert land than with a contentious and fretful woman." A woman cannot endure her life if she can't come to peace with her mate.

Sarai might have forgiven Abram because she knew that he had been frightened and had acted out of weakness. A man, even a brave man, could have a momentary lapse, a time of moral frailty.

❧

I imagine that she forgave him because she did not have a choice.

Sarai accepted her place the way she accepted the rain on the tent flap. She could manage well enough despite the harness of her gender.

At a time of danger an angel had come to save her. She must have felt privileged to be the wife of Abram.

Abram returned to the land of the Canaanites a man of wealth and substance. He had silver and gold in his chest. He had more camels and slaves than ever before. A story is told that he had been given a costly robe with rubies and ropes of pearls. Sarai must have seen all this. But she must have had another gift in mind, a reward from God for the terrible night she had spent in Pharaoh's bed. Now perhaps she would conceive a child.

Farther and farther, day after day, they traveled back into Canaan.

There was rain. There was grass enough for the sheep to birth lambs, and the cows gave milk. Everyone Abram met on the way listened to him talk about the one true God, about the falseness of idols, about the need to praise only Eloheim, the one who had spoken to Abram. Many of those he talked with believed him. Even those who didn't remembered his words and repeated them to others.

Sarai did not conceive.

They traveled along with Lot and his wife and their children and all they had to the Negev, where the grass was high and the new lambs nibbled at the roots of the wild onions. They must have found water here and there, a small stream, an abandoned well where the camels, bending their knobby knees, slid down the steep sides and drank from the pool below. In the morning bees flew above the bushes. Abram's servants smashed the hives in the evening and the women drained the honey into clay jars.

Slowly they made their way to the place between Bethel and Ai, where Abram had built an altar, and when he found the altar just as he had left it, he called out to the Lord and praised him for all he had given him.

Sarai might have walked out into the field behind the camp. She might have stood alone on a small mound made of dirt and rocks, seeing charred wood and small pieces of stone. Who had been there before? She saw where the embers had burnt the grass. Sarai would have prayed to God to grant her a child. It was an old prayer. God had heard it many times. She must have tried to find a new way to speak to Eloheim of her need. How would He hear her over all the noises of the earth, over all the cries and moans of the sick and the dying, over the whisperings of male and female? How could she make sure that He would see her, standing alone, apart, in need? All the words she used to entreat God must have become stale in her mouth, drained of life, limp.

Maybe she began to hum. She hoped God would see her there. Would God take pity on her? She stayed there until the darkness fell all around her and clouds blocked the stars. She stayed there until she could stay no longer.

᭞

ot too had been enriched by the stay in Egypt. Abram had given him a portion of the pharaoh's gifts. Lot had tended his flocks with care. They had increased many times over. He had tents for his servants, and his household had many mouths that required feeding. The land where Abram now stayed could not support all these people, all these animals. The servants of Abram were quarreling with the servants of Lot about the use of a well, about the use of a hill, about the stealing of barley, one from another.

Maybe Sarai was jealous of Lot's wife. She had daughters, little girls who followed her about as she walked over the fields. What has she done to make her more deserving of God's favor than I? Sarai may have thought. The sight of the little girls, who smiled and waved at her when they would see her on the path, made her sad.

Rav. Chaninah ben Pazzi said, "Lot's daughters, like thorns, conceived easily. The Matriarchs, like wheat, endured much before it happened." That rabbi understood Sarai's suffering.

It would be better if Lot and his household moved away from us, Sarai may have thought.

enesis 13 tells us that the land as far as the eye could see could not contain all their animals, all their people. The herdsmen of Lot and the herdsmen of Abram fought with one another. Each accused the other of taking more than their share of the water to feed his animals. In Genesis 13:8, "And Abram said to Lot, 'Let there be no contention between you and me, between your herdsmen and mine, for we are kinsmen. Is not all the land before you? Pray, let us part company. If you take the right hand, I shall go left.'" Lot saw the whole plain of the Jordan and saw that it was green and water flowed through it all. Lot may have thought he saw the Lord's first garden. He chose for himself the whole plain of the Jordan, and he gathered his wife and his young daughters and he folded up his tents and moved eastward away from Abram toward the city of Sodom.

Sarai may not have regretted this separation.

I imagine Sarai moves about her daily tasks wanting and wanting what she now believes she will never have.

One day perhaps the end of days will be upon us and the Messiah will come and every woman who wants to conceive a child will do so and every child who needs a mother will have one.

Abram and Sarai stood on a hill and watched as Lot and his people grew smaller and smaller in their eyes and the distance between them grew so great that at last no matter how hard they stared at the horizon's edge they could no longer see any people or cattle. Then Sarai went to gather the berries that grew in thickets nearby.

*I*n Genesis 13:14–16 the Lord appeared to Abram again and said, "Raise your eyes and look out from the place where you

are to the north and the south and the east and the west, for all
the land you see, to you I will give it and to your seed forever
and I will make your seed like the dust of the earth." The Lord
told Abram to walk about the land, for it was his, granted to
him by his Creator. Walking about the perimeter of property
was a common legal ritual in the ancient Near East for taking
final possession. The conveyance of property was expressed in
this manner in Ugaritic texts composed in the fourteenth and
thirteenth centuries B.C.E.

In the following days Abram took up his tent and came to
the great oaks of Mamre, which are in Hebron. Some sages say
that Mamre is the navel of the world. There Abram built another altar to the Lord.

*I*f only all the others in the land had been as peaceful in their
hearts, as devoted to the Creator of the world as Abram, then
perhaps there would have been no need for armies and swords
and the trampling of bodies and spilling of blood.

But a messenger came riding up to the tents of Abram and
Sarai. The instant Sarai saw him appearing at the far edge of
the meadow she must have been uneasy. It may have been as
some sages say that Sarai had the gift of prophecy and could
see the future before it arrived, or maybe the approach of
strangers was rare and anyone who was not of your family
could intend grave harm. The messenger spoke to Abram in a
soft voice and Sarai could not make out his words. Abram told
her that his nephew Lot—who was also her cousin—with
all his family had been taken prisoner by Amraphe, king of

Shinar; Arioch, king of Ellasar; Cheedorlaomer, king of Elam; and Tidal, king of Goim. These warlords had attacked Sodom and Gomorrah. The warlords had themselves been subjected to taxes and tariffs and raids for many years. Now they rebelled, and all through the valley of Siddim there were armed clashes between the men of one group and the men of another. Abram must have told Sarai that the kings of Sodom and Gomorrah fled into the bitumen pits and had hidden in the black coal and so had evaded capture.

Sarai must have known as she heard this that Abram would call his men together and they would mount their camels and gather their supplies and pursue the warlords who had captured Lot. She might have made an attempt to stop him. But he went. His brother's child was like his child. He must care for his own.

Sarai watched Abram ride off. Three hundred men were with him. I imagine that all the wives stood at the edge of the meadow and waved. Some had children on their hips. The children cried. For many days and nights Sarai must have waited, walked to the top of the nearest hill and searched for any sign of Abram's return. Penelope sat at her loom for twenty years waiting for Ulysses to return. Sarai did not have to suffer for so long.

Fear must have invaded Sarai's mind. She must have imagined Abram with blood spilling out of his chest, blood seeping into the ground. She must have imagined the tribes tying him up, shaving his head, forcing him into hard labor. She could have seen herself a captive in another kingdom. She would have said nothing to her servants, making sure that the cows were milked and the goats were grazed and the dog that slept at the tent door had his share of the lamb. She would have kneaded the dough from the grain that they had stored. Whether or not Abram returned, Sarai would have known that sorrow would come to the land because men on all sides would fall in battle and the dead would leave behind empty beds. There would be weeping when it was all over. It was hard to understand how Abram's God permitted this draining of blood on His beautiful land. He should not have allowed it. Could not the Creator of all things have turned men's hearts away from war?

After some time passed Sarai would have stopped reproaching Abram for his war or asking further questions of the Lord. She would have grown quiet inside, patient, stilled. What would happen could not be changed by her wishes or her prayers or her imaginings, dark or otherwise. She hardly ate. She hardly slept. She simply waited.

Abram returned victorious. He would have reported to Sarai how he had surrounded the kings at night and his men had slashed their way to the center of the enemy camp and how Lot had greeted him with joy and how he had pursued his enemies all the way to Hobah, which is north of Damascus, and he brought back the spoils but had given everything to his allies and allowed only the men who had served with him to take a share.

There is a story repeated in the collection *Hebrew Myths* by Robert Graves and Raphael Patai that when Abram had come up in the night to the enemy camp the planet Jupiter shed a mysterious light around him, a light that only his own army could see, so the others groping in blackness were easily defeated. It was also said that Layla, the angel of the night, assisted him, leading him here and there, lifting him up above the dangers. Many stories are told about that battle. They say that the swords of the enemy turned to dust as they raised them, ready to slash at Abram's men. They say that when Abram lost his javelin in the fray he picked up a handful of dust and threw it at his foes, and instantly the dust become a dozen javelins. Another tale: when Abram threw straw in the air it became a volley of arrows.

All around the land of Canaan and into Ur and up through Egypt, elaborate long epic stories were told of heroes and their battles and their gods, who when bribed with proper sacrifice fought on one side or another. Abram's battle, this little battle, was disposed of in the book of Genesis in a few lines. Those to whom these words are sacred did not admire military skills as much as they might.

Several rabbis have remarked on the fact that the book of Genesis reports on warfare but is not about war. It does not dwell on the details of battle as other founding stories do. It focuses on Abram's moral quality and the ethical issues that test man. Wars come and go through the book of Genesis, but they are not the point.

After Abram told Sarai the story of his battle it's likely he never again referred to it.

A legend tells us that King Melchizedek, who fought on Abram's side, was actually his ancestor Shem, the same Shem that is said to have opened a great academy of learning, and that he had given Abram the garments of skin made by God for Adam and Eve that had been stolen by Ham.

❧

*G*enesis 15:5 tells us that Abram had a night vision. He must have told Sarai all that he had seen and heard. God said to Abram, "Look up at the heavens and count the stars, if you can count them." And He said, "So shall be your seed." And God said to Abram, "I am the Lord your God who brought you out of Ur of the Chaldees to give you this land to inherit." And Abram made a covenant with the Lord in which he took a three-year-old heifer and a three-year-old she goat and a three-year-old ram and a turtledove and a young pigeon and he split the animals in half. Abram fell into a deep sleep, and then when the sun had set, a blazing torch appeared in a brazier and came between the cleft animals. The sages say that the turtledove was the nation that would come from Ishmael, the child that Hagar would bear for Abram, and the pigeon who in life made his home in the rocks above the rivers was Israel, the nation that would come from Abram and Sari. Those two birds were not severed in the making of this covenant. The mysterious holy flame that had moved between the parts of the animals was another kind of fire, a purification of the offering, a sign of divine power, a holy sign of God's presence at the scene. This is an echo of the fire that burned in the furnace but did not burn Abram.

Sarai was not present at the making of this covenant. But it concerned her too.

In the Tanhuma Shoftim (the book of Judges) there is a story that God lifted Abram above the dome of heaven and said, "Look at the stars and try to count them—whoever stands beneath a star fears it, but you seeing one shine below may now lift up your head consider yourself greater than the stars." Sarai without a child most likely did not consider herself great or greatly loved by God.

A story tells us that Azazel, the fallen angel, or Satan as he came to be called, was disguised as a vulture to feast on the carcasses of the sacrificed animals. But Abram's guardian angel said to Azazel, "What do you here, on these holy heights where no mortal may eat or drink? Fly off lest heavenly powers burn you. Abram's lot lies on the heights as yours lies in the depths. Depart for you can never lead him astray."

I add this: Sarai may have asked, "What does Azazel look like?" "He is like me," said Abram, "but not like me." "What is different about him?" asked Sarai. "Perhaps he is taller and his beard is fuller and his chest is wider," said Abram.

And I add this: Sarai was amazed at Abram's report. "Did God name me?" she asked. "Did He say that I would be the mother of the nation?" Abram was silent. "Who then?" asked Sarai, a tightness in her chest. "I did not ask," said Abram, "but you are my wife, my only wife." He comforted her by stroking her hair, which by now was streaked with gray. She fell asleep but awoke remembering that God had not mentioned her, not by name.

Sarai must have thought, I am never going to have a child.

She may have said to herself, I am the Lord's servant. I will accept his will. Saying this was easy; believing it could not have been. Genesis 16:3 tells us that Sarai took her slave Hagar who had been given to her by Pharaoh and brought her to Abram so that through Hagar Abram could have a child to fulfill the promises of God, Abram's God, not hers.

This was a common practice among the peoples of the land. In the laws of Hammurabi it tells us that "if Gilimnina bears her husband Shennima children, he will not take another wife. But if Gilimnia is unfruitful, it is she who will choose a woman for her husband." It was also said that if a priestess who is bound not to have children of her own gives a slave to her husband, and if after the birth of a child the slave demands equal honor with her mistress, then she cannot be sold but she can be returned to bondage among her female slaves. It is strangely comforting that there were domestic comedies, domestic tragedies even in the homes of priestesses.

The name Hagar means "village" in South Arabic. This means that Hagar was carrying the hopes of those in all the small villages that Abram and his tribe passed on their journey. She has entered the story from another side, tying together all the peoples of the land, those who joined with Abram and those who did not.

I imagine it this way: the dates were spread out on the ground, left to bake and dry in the sun. Sarai and her servants pressed the ripe dates and gathered the sweet juices into bowls. The well was high with water. The palm fronds were stripped from the trees and woven into baskets and ropes. Abram came one night into Hagar's tent. He woke her from her sleep. She understood when he lay beside her.

I imagine that Sarai lay in her tent on her pallet while her husband lay with her slave. She could not hear them. The slaves' tent was at a distance from her own, but sleep did not come. Maybe it was raining. Maybe the sound of rain continued through the night. Maybe Sarai pulled the cover off her body because she was too warm and then she became cold and shivered as she pushed away the images in her mind of the slave on the bed with her husband. It was not unusual for a man to take a second or even a third wife or several concubines, but Abram had never expressed a wish for another beside her. He now took Hagar into his arms, and it had been Sarai's suggestion, her sacrifice.

A woman learns to put her husband before herself. But at a price. It was likely that Sarai's beautiful face lost its shine. There were dark shadows under her eyes and her lips were pulled tight together.

Immediately Hagar conceived.

She would not do Sarai's bidding without complaint. She ignored her commands. Genesis 16 says, "And he came to bed with Hagar and she conceived and she saw that she had conceived and her mistress seemed slight in her eyes." Imagine Hagar as she steals Sarai's favorite shawl and wears it in front of her. Who can blame Hagar for some preening and boasting. A slave is without choice. A slave uses up her days in the service of others, the washing, the folding, the dirtiest tasks, the most tedious of daily chores and all without reward or hope of reward. A slave is not fully a person in anyone else's eyes. But a slave has a soul that yearns. Hagar was once a princess in her father's house. True, legend tells us she was also the daughter of a concubine, but even so she must have been given presents, worn fine clothes, had a servant who bathed her and combed her hair.

Then the strangers came down from Canaan and her father delivered her into their hands. How lonely it must have been without her own mother, without her companions in the palace. Here she worked through the day and slept on the hard earth. A sage reported that she was forced to ride a limping donkey when they moved to the greener lands, and her fine hands had grown sores from washing. As a girl she may have played the harp. Here in the fields she never sang. I think of her as small and quiet. Who would listen to her? And then at last Hagar is given an opportunity to achieve the one thing her mistress cannot.

There is a legend that the women of the nearby tribes came to visit Sarai and they talked about the one true God for a while and then Sarai asked them to visit Hagar, perhaps in hopes that she would praise her mistress before them. But Hagar said to the women, "Sarai is not what she seems to be. Outwardly she makes the impression of a righteous, pious woman, but she is not, for if she were how could her childlessness be explained after so many years of marriage while I became pregnant at once." This cruel remark reminds us that infertility was assumed to be God's punishment for a sin of deed or thought.

Of course at least one of the women repeated these words to Sarai, who said nothing, but now she perceived Hagar as her enemy. Now she had no kind feelings for her slave who was her rival in her husband's eyes and in God's eyes. And her anger could no longer be contained.

✲

After that the story takes another turn, a turn that will lead down dark roads in future time.

In Genesis 16 we read that Sarai said to Abram, "This outrage against me is because of you! I myself put my slave girl in your embrace and when she saw she had conceived I became slight in her eyes. Let the Lord judge between you and me." Abram said to Sarai, "Look, your slave girl is in your hands. Do to her whatever you think right."

This may seem an ordinary matter, a thing of jealousy, a husband stepping aside, letting his wife do as she wished, expressing his greater loyalty to Sarai than to the concubine who was bearing his child, but this is more than domestic chatter. A chasm opens here, an opportunity for peace between opposing parties is lost, a moment in which both women lose their moral center, for which mankind will pay in rivers of blood.

Sarai begins to humiliate Hagar. The sages tell us that Sarai makes Hagar clean the tent again and again. Sarai takes the clothes that Hagar had washed and throws them in the dirt. She calls her slave a sloth in front of all the household. She spits in her food and then orders Hagar to eat it. The sages report that Sarai takes her slippers and throws them in Hagar's face. (Throwing a shoe across property was then a way of declaring ownership.) Hagar was tired and perhaps nauseated from the first weeks of her pregnancy. Sarai told her to stay out of doors, to tend the animals after dark, to sit alone when others were eating. She forced Hagar to follow behind her with pails and towels to the bathhouse, shaming her servant by forcing her to watch her mistress clean herself.

Sarah's mistreatment of Hagar became more than the slave could bear. I imagine she must have been exhausted and probably afraid that Sarai might in her anger even harm her one night, slash at her belly, destroy the child within.

Hagar fled from the tents of Abraham. Here is this expectant mother, without a friend in the universe, with family miles and miles away, with no one to call her name or hold her hand. How many women have been pregnant alone in the millennia that followed, and all of them afraid. If such fear could start a drought, the earth would have become barren rock centuries ago.

The Lord took pity. Or the Lord had other plans, designs of his own that led his creations further into the drama that was unfolding.

A messenger of the Lord found Hagar by a spring of water in the wilderness on the way to Shur at the border with Egypt. Perhaps she was intending to throw herself on her father's mercy. Perhaps she had no plan at all. Genesis 16:10 tells us that the angel said to her, "Return to your mistress and suffer harassment at her hands. I will surely multiply your seed and it will be beyond all counting." The messenger told her, "Look you have conceived a son and you will call his name Ishmael for the Lord has heeded your suffering. And he will be a wild ass of a man—his hand against the hand of all against him." The name Ishmael means "God has heard." The well that she stopped by was named Beer Lahai Roi. It means something like Well of the Living One Who Sees Me.

Hagar must have been grateful that she had not died in the encounter with the messenger of God. It was thought at the time that all who came into the presence of the Holy One would die instantly. So fearful was man that he was unworthy of God, so sure he was that his metal was base and his soul such a little thing, that it would burn up in the heat of divinity.

Some sages say that Sarai cursed Hagar and Hagar lost her fetus, which was a female, in the desert and only conceived her son after her return to Abram. Perhaps. It does says in *B. Niddah*, one of the commentaries on the text, that there is an angel appointed over every pregnancy. Perhaps this angel saved Hagar's fetus or at least comforted her if she lost her daughter. But either way curses come from the mouths of witches, and Sarai was not a witch—she was simply a barren woman who had, through infertility, lost the right to claim her husband's exclusive attention. No doubt she hated Hagar and wished her and her fetus dead, but wishes do not alter facts.

Hagar was missing for many days. Abram must have sent his goatherds out to find her, but they returned without her. I imagine that he himself rode out north and south, calling her name, but she did not answer. He thought perhaps she had been eaten by a wild lion or taken by a boar and pierced by his tusks. I imagine he did not talk to Sarai or come to her tent at night. He prayed to the Lord to protect his concubine. A man is capable of more than one love. Sarai would have seen that he grieved for Hagar and Hagar's child and she might have been afraid he would never return to her.

But after the angel spoke to her in the wilderness Hagar

returned to Sarai and endured her cruelty, and when her time came she gave birth to a son, Abram's child, Ishmael.

Abram was eighty-six years old when his first son was born.

I imagine that he took the baby in his arms and walked down to the camels. "Here," he said, "is a camel, here," he said, "is a sheep." He must have thanked his God. Sarai most probably did not hold the baby. She would not have looked at this child as it learned to roll over on the mat. This baby could not have pleased her.

A rabbi in the seventh century said, "When Sarah persecuted Hagar she committed a sin." In the twelfth century Moses Ben Nachman, known as Nachmanides, said the sufferings of the Jewish people derive from those that Sarai inflicted on Hagar. Another twelfth-century Jewish philosopher Rabbi David Kimhi added that "Sarah should be blamed for her immoral behavior, her lack of charity and compassion. The words 'And she, Sarah, made her suffer'—haunt the history of Israel." The Redak, another sage of the twelfth century, said, "God did not approve of what Sarah had done, and this entire story has been transcribed in the Torah in order to teach people good qualities and to remove evil qualities." According to the Redak, Sarai's behavior toward Hagar is considered a moral example of how people should not behave toward one another. The Ramban said, "Sarah our mother sinned in dealing harshly with her handmaid and Abraham too by allowing her to do so."

Elie Wiesel, speaking of Sarai's harshness to Hagar, asks, "What about pity, and compassion and the human heart—?"

*I*f Moses Maimonides could critizice Abram for asking Sarai to say he was her brother, then surely it is possible that Sarai's treatment of Hagar was an error of tragic proportions. But the mother of us all was not a saint, not a person of such overwhelming goodness of spirit that she could overlook the painful slight that she had suffered. She could not or did not choose to reproach her God, who had not filled her own womb with life. She did not blame her husband that he took a concubine. He did not do so until she herself offered Hagar to him. Her anger turned against another woman, one more helpless than herself.

*T*hirteen years passed, and Ishmael grew into a strong boy. I imagine he must have avoided Sarai as much as possible; perhaps he could feel her eyes on his back when he tossed stones in the ditch, when he jumped over the basket of berries that had been left on the rock. He must have tried smiling at her, and maybe he once brought her a snail he had found at the edge of the stream. She would have brushed away his hand. Ishmael may have ducked behind trees, laid flat in the dirt, covered himself with the flap of a tent, with the skin of a sheep when he saw Sarai. When the entire camp traveled north in the warm weather, south in the heat, he may have made sure his donkey was at the rear of the family, that he was out of Sarai's vision.

He would have brought his mother the ripest pomegranate. He must have brought his mother baskets of figs.

I imagine that Sarai grew gray and now there were only a few strands of her black hair left. Her skin was wrinkled and her mouth had lost its firm lines. The muscles of her arms were still strong and she could walk as far as a young woman, but her eyes could not see clearly, and sometimes she almost walked into a log or stumbled into a bramble. Her monthly bleeding had long ago stopped, and with that she had become dry and often her skin was hot. She still loved Abram. Often she must have forgotten she was old altogether and laughed with her handmaidens.

When at the end of the summer there was no longer green grass for the animals and they packed everything up and moved, she rode with Abram at the front of the line. He must have looked on her with pride. She must have known that he still found her worthy of his affection. The sweetness of the world filled her heart and she thanked Abram's God for the good that appeared everywhere in her life. And if she still was bitter that she had never had a child she may have hidden that bitterness even from herself.

It says in Genesis 17 that Abram was ninety-nine years old when the Lord appeared to him again. This time He told Abram to change his name to Abraham and He promised him again that he would be a father to nations. And He promised him the land, the whole land of Canaan as an everlasting holding. He commanded Abraham to circumcise the flesh of his foreskin and to do the same to all the males that traveled with him, even slaves or those purchased from any foreigner. The Lord changed Sarai's name to Sarah, and He promised that kings of peoples should issue from her.

It says in Genesis 16:16 when Abraham heard this he flung himself on his face and he laughed, saying to himself, "To a hundred-year-old will a child be born, will ninety-year-old Sarah give birth?"

Then Abraham said to the Lord, "Would that Ishmael might live in your favor." A sage said that Abraham was afraid that Ishmael would die if Sarah was to have a son, and Abraham loved his son Ishmael.

Abraham did as the Lord told him. He cut his foreskin and the foreskin of all the males around him, including thirteen-year-old Ishmael. This circumcision was a far better blood-letting than the more common practice of human sacrifice. We have reports that the tribes around Abraham had offered their small children to their gods in hopes of evoking good fortune. Large graveyards have been found with the buried bones of tiny children assumed to have been sacrificed at the dawn of human history. Abraham's God asked only a small piece of the foreskin as a token of loyalty. The custom of circumcision may have come to replace the sacrifice of infants. The act of circumcision allows a group to give to their God only a small bit of flesh in place of the whole child.

After the circumcision the men were in pain. There must have been blood in the grass where the cutting took place.

I imagine that Sarah may have wondered about this strange act that the Lord had asked of Abraham. Men are not animals to be sacrificed to the Lord. How can this be? Women bleed because we are so designed, but men should not bleed. Why did God ask this?

The arguments for and against circumcision continue. What we do know is that the act of cutting the foreskin of the male infant at eight days after birth has stayed with large numbers of human beings over the millennia. It is a tribal mark, a linking of the generations back to Abraham. It is a way to separate those of one group from another. This separation binds one group to its members, but it also makes clear who belongs and who doesn't. It makes the circumcised a target for the uncircumcised or the other way around.

There is no record of Sarah's objections to this ritual.

Great stories from other groups tell of fathers eating their children, of fathers killing their children. This small cut of the foreskin may also be a way to hold the envy of the generations one against the other in check.

Abraham himself cut Ishmael, who was thirteen years old at the time, telling him that he was now marked for the Lord. I imagine that Ishmael felt Abraham's hand on his thigh and he was soothed. I imagine that Sarah went into her tent and refused to minister to the men whose wound, although small, was still painful. "Let the Lord's angels take care of them," she may have said. Abraham did not tell her that the Lord had said she would bear him a child. He may have been afraid his words would be salt in her wound, that she would turn away from him and perhaps from God himself in her anger.

I imagine that the next day Sarah relented and she brought bread and honey and the juice of lemons to the men as they lay on their pallets. The next day she thanked the Lord for all his kindness. The next day she went visiting the men. She may even have given Ishmael a drink from the water pitcher, but she would not have looked at him, not even if he thanked her and called her his mistress.

Under the great trees of Mamre the Lord appeared to Abraham three days later as Abraham was sitting in his tent watching the road. Genesis 18 tells us that Abraham looked out and saw three men, and he begged them to stop by so he could bring them sustenance. He offered them the shade of the largest tree, and he hurried to Sarah and asked her to bake the bread from their best flour and he went to the herdsman and selected a perfect calf. And the three men, who the sages say were actually the three angels Gabriel and Michael and Raphael, spoke to Abraham. They asked him, "Where is Sarah your wife?" And Abraham told them she was there in the tent. The angel Raphael said, "I will return to you at this very season and your wife will have a son in her arms, her own son." Sarah was listening at the tent flap and Sarah laughed to herself saying, "After being shriveled, shall I have pleasure and my husband is old? Shall I really give birth old as I am." I imagine she looked down at the blue veins in her hands. She may have felt the ache in her shoulder that came each day after she had lifted the pitchers of milk. She knew that her hair was thin and gray. I am dust, she might have thought to herself. My time for a child is gone. I believe that she thought this and did not weep. She thought this without self-pity.

I imagine there was no mirth in her laughter, that it sounded like a spoon scraping on a tin plate. It would have been a bitter laugh. We laugh sometimes when we want to cry. She may not have been pleased by this promise of a belated gift.

And the Lord said to Abraham, "Why is it that Sarah laughed, saying, Shall I really give birth, old as I am? Is anything beyond the Lord?" Sarah heard God's words from the opening in the tent where she was standing. Sarah lied to the Lord. "I did not laugh," she said, because she was afraid. And the Lord said to her, "Yes, you did laugh."

The sages say that the Lord said to Sarah, since you laughed you will name your son Isaac, which means "laughter."

Rashi noticed that the Lord did not tell Abraham Sarah's exact words. He kept from the husband the wife's claim that her husband was old. The Lord, in addition to creating all the creatures of the earth, understood that tact would spare Abraham the harsh facts of his age and protect the bond between Sarah and her husband.

I assume that Sarah knew that she was old and her husband was old and the birth of a child would be unnatural. According to the book of Judges she cried out, "Is it possible that this womb shall bear a child and that these dried-up breasts shall give forth milk." She had not been waiting for her dead womb to wake. But she would have been ashamed that she had laughed and even more ashamed that she had tried to deny it. If she could relive that moment and prevent that laugh from entering her mind, she would, but the moment had come and gone so quickly. The laugh had been so insistent, so determined, like a tornado. The Lord did not sound angry when he spoke to her. But was he angry? Would he take back his promise because she had laughed? She could not hope for the impossible, but in a corner of her mind she considered the coming of a child, the warmth of its body, the feel of its fingers in her fingers. The Lord can do anything, even change the human body, break the common laws of age and death, she may have told herself. If only I hadn't laughed.

Sarah must have wondered, Could the Lord be so cruel as to promise me a child only to mock me? She may have looked up at the stars in the sky, at the moon moving in its usual orbit. Why should the Lord care about her?

The angels Gabriel, Michael, and Raphael had come to earth for several reasons. The sages say that Gabriel was to comfort Abraham in his pain, and that Michael was to inform Sarah that she would bear a child, and that Raphael's mission was to destroy the cities of Sodom and Gomorrah.

Abraham was told by God that the cities of the plain would soon be consumed in fire and brimstone. Abraham tried to convince God to spare the cities. He argued with him about the numbers of good men that might be living there. What number would be sufficient for God to hold back his fury, one hundred, eighty, ten? In the end God decided only to save Lot and his family for the sake of Abraham. The good men that Abraham claimed worthy of life seemed not to exist. Sarah was not a part of this conversation with God. But Abraham must have told her immediately that the destruction was at hand. Abraham must have told her he tried to save the cities and failed. She may have comforted him with her hands, with kind looks, with a drink of fresh water.

She surely understood that God had appeared in their lives, a great and awesome presence, and she must have felt amazed, the dress she was wearing, the pitcher made of clay by her knee, the branch of the oak tree, everything near must have seemed graced by the closeness of the Creator.

For several years Sarah and Abraham had received messages from Sodom and Gomorrah that were hard to believe, so brutal were the stories, so cruel seemed the citizens of those cities. Abraham always offered comfort to those who wandered past his tents, but those in Sodom and Gomorrah tormented and tortured those who came their way. The sages tell us terrible stories about the people of the wicked cities. Sarah must have had tears in her eyes when she heard how the Sodomites had placed a stranger in a bed far too small for him and tied his legs to the posts until his bones broke and he died. She heard that if a stranger was small they stretched him out on a large bed and tied him to the four posts until he was torn apart.

Stories like those told about Sodom are repeated in other cultures, centuries away in time, miles away in geography. Procrustes the Innkeeper was killed by Theseus, the king of Athens, for using such a bed to torture his guests to death. Did the Greeks steal this story from the Hebrews? Several sages tell the story that one of the daughters of Sodom took pity on a wandering minstrel and gave him food and drink, and as a punishment the townspeople stripped her of her clothes and covered her in honey and buried her in an ant nest until she died of a myriad bites. Her cries of pain reached the heavens, and the sages say that was the last straw, the one that prompted the Lord to punish the citizens of Sodom and Gomorrah and put an end to their vile acts.

Sarah must have heard that all strangers who entered the city gates were robbed of their possessions and that men were often raped in the gates of the city by crowds of other men. She must have heard that women were consumed alive by being placed in barrels with hungry rats. The sources tell us that Lot's oldest daughter, Palit, had brought a blanket to a stranger at the gates on a night when frost was in the air. She was buried alive. These stories were all hard to believe.

I imagine this: "How could they?" Sarah asked of her maidservant. "They could," the maidservant replied. The girl, who may have been taken slave as a child, had seen many terrible things.

It was said by one of the sages that in the fields outside of Sodom, gold, silver, pearls, and diamonds lay about in abundance in the grass, and the inhabitants of the city had only to walk a little way to pick up the jewels, and all of the citizens were rich beyond imagining. It was this wealth that made the people of Sodom and Gomorrah merciless toward others. It was this wealth they were hiding from strangers' eyes.

Sarah knew that travelers had good reasons for their journeys, and after long days moving from place to place they had human needs that should be succored. God would want this for all His human creatures, so must Sarah have thought, who found the tales of horror coming from the plains almost unbearable. She knew that her cousin Lot and his family were down there among the others. Lot had never been the most honest or truthful of men, but he would never turn his back on the needs of a stranger. He too was a follower of the one true God.

The sky turned pink in the East, and Abraham and Sarah stood under the skeleton white moon and looked down into the plains of Jordan. The Lord's promise to Sarah would not have been discussed.

I imagine that they saw a pillar of smoke at the edge of the horizon. The smoke rose up to meet the floating clouds. Abraham walked out on the field, staring all the while at the pink glow that was coming clearer. The sky clouded over and rain fell, but in the rain was ash, a burning smell came over all. Abraham and Sarah took refuge under a tree. They held each other close, seeing the anger of the Lord rising so many miles away. Abraham may have wondered about his nephew. Abraham may have longed to go down to the plains to search for him. Meteors appeared in the distance, fire-breathing stones were falling on the cities of the plain. Down below they saw the pools of fire growing and glowing. Sarah may again have wished she hadn't laughed.

The meteors still fell from the sky, but the earth had stopped trembling. Some ewes had given birth before their time. Slowly the sun came out from behind the dark clouds and the wind blew away the smell of smoke and burning. Sarah saw that it was done. She saw that the Lord did what he said he would do. Sarah must have begun to hope. The Lord had also made promises to her.

Perhaps a messenger came who had been living outside of Zoar. He told Abraham and Sarah that Lot and his daughters had escaped with the help of an angel. I imagine that the messenger told them that Lot's wife had looked back for her married daughters, even though she had been forbidden to look behind her, and she had been turned into a pillar of salt. Sarah would have been truly sad. She too would have looked back for her children. She too would never have obeyed a command to leave them without turning around. She knew this, even though she had no children.

Did God want a woman to leave her child as if it were a bundle of broken dishes? Did God understand how firmly a woman was bound to the child of her womb?

Abraham would have been pleased that the earth still contained his nephew, that God had spared him. He would not waste time in mourning over the Cities of Sin, which had turned their back on the Lord and played with human life as if it had no worth at all. Sarah may have thought of the children in Sodom and Gomorrah who had not yet learned to hate God. I assume she understood that God had to take the innocent along with the guilty to create an example for the generations to come.

Rashi said that the Lord had destroyed Sodom and Gomorrah at dawn right at the line between night and day so that the people of the land would not think that their false sun god had accomplished such a thing and they would not think that their false moon god had the power to destroy a city. Not everyone believed in the one true God. The idol worshippers were many and they offered the first fruits of their harvest to local gods made of wood and stone. Anthropologists and archaeologists tell us that in those days anxious human hands tied lambs to branches of trees, spilled their blood, and burnt them to please their gods.

After the destruction of Sodom and Gomorrah the rains once more held back. The sky was clear without a cloud. Abraham and Sarah decided to travel to Gerar, where the grass would still be green and the water flowed blue in the rivers and the wells were easy to find.

I imagine as they set out on this journey Sarah felt a familiar surge in her body. She ran to a grove of trees and saw that her time of month had returned. How was this possible? Her skin was not smooth, the molar on her left side had fallen away. Her arms must have been freckled and her breasts too low. She knew all this but she saw that her body had given her back a trace of her youth. Perhaps others would follow.

A sage claimed that as they traveled to Gerar each day Sarah became more radiant. The blackness in her hair returned. He skin became smooth. Her lips regained their firm line. Her legs were strong. She looked in the stream and saw herself and was amazed. She looked at Abraham, and he too regained the firm line of his jaw, the thickness of his hair, the rolling muscles in his arms and legs. They embraced as if they had just met, as if the years of their life had hardly begun. Abraham and Sarah journeyed on to the Negev, which was green with summer grass, and settled their camp between Kadesh and Shur.

I imagine a new well with its sloping sides was dug and the animals were soon watered. Sarah found that she could carry a pitcher on her shoulder all the way down and all the way up without resting. This she had not been able to do in a long time.

Sarah must not have been able to prevent the regret that rose in her heart, taste of bile and rue, when a child of a servant addressed her as "aunt" or "mistress." She watched the children as they gathered the beans in the field. She saw their brown legs and their quick fingers, and the yearning returned.

When they came to Gerar they saw King Abimelech's men approaching. In Genesis 20 Abraham for the second time asked Sarah to say she was his sister. This time she must have trusted that she would be protected from harm. And she was.

A sage points out that while it is a sin to lie it is sometimes the only way that the powerless can survive in the face of the strength opposing them. He claims that lying is not always wrong if the purpose is to assure the survival of the nation. Without some trickery all Israel would have fallen out of the human story. There are many tricks in the stories to come. Without them, disaster.

I imagine Sarah was now taken to Abimelech's palace, which stood by a flowing stream and was guarded by his soldiers, who stood in the shade of two great oaks. The stone walls around the palace were covered in honeysuckle vines and the air smelled sweet. Abram was shown to his quarters, and food was brought to him on a gold platter. He prayed to the

Lord to protect his wife. His prayer was sincere, but his anxiety was not as great as when Sarah had disappeared into Pharaoh's dwelling. His own arms were useless. He was one man against many. Sarah was brought to Abimelech's private rooms. She waited for him there. His will was strong, and all who lived inside his walls did his bidding without question or complaint. But the sages tell us that as the night wore on a strange spell fell on all the people in his dwelling except for Abraham and Sarah. All their orifices were closed up. Their bodies could no longer lose their wastes. They could no longer smell, nor open their mouths except to moan. The wombs of the women were closed shut and the men's genitals became wrinkled and shriveled. There was a great cry of pain from every corner of the palace. The women were weeping and the men were hitting the walls with their fists. "What is it, what is happening?" they cried. A legend tells us that the Angel Michael stood by Abimelech's bed with a sword and struck him in the back of his neck as he approached Sarah. Abimelech let out a cry, fell forward on the bed, and dropped like a stone from a great height into a deep sleep. In Genesis 20:4 it says that in a night dream Abimelech heard God's voice. It said, "You are a dead man because of the woman you took, as she belongs to another man."

Abimelech protested that he was innocent. He had not touched her. He thought she was the sister of the stranger. God said to Abimelech, "Send back the man's wife, for he is a prophet and will intercede for you and you may live. If you do not send her back know that you are doomed to die, you and all that belongs to you."

Legend tells us that at dawn the soldiers and guards, the

courtiers and their wives, gathered outside Abimelech's chamber and called to him, "One more night like last night and we shall all be dead." Abimelech woke from his sleep and ordered Sarah to leave his room and go back to her husband.

Abimelech gave Abraham oxen, sheep, and a thousand pieces of silver and told him to settle in the land wherever he wished. Sarah may again have been angry with Abraham because again he had put his own life above hers.

Genesis 20:18 tells us that the Lord had rescued Sarah by closing up the wombs of Abimelech's women and preventing the men from creating life. This way of preserving Sarah's honor demonstrated to all that Sarah had not been violated and that the child who would later issue from her womb carried Abraham's, not Abimelech's, seed.

I imagine that for many weeks Sarah would not let Abraham enter her tent. It says in Proverbs 16:7, "When a Man's ways please the Lord he maketh even his enemies to be at peace with him." Rabbi Yohanon said, "In this passage, the word enemy refers to a man's wife." So Sarah forgave and embraced Abraham. His mind quieted, and he was pleased.

I imagine that Sarah's time of the month did not come when she expected it. Was age coming back on her? Was the miracle over? Sarah may have felt tenderness in her breasts. She may have believed that the sun was too hot and she was weak and she took to her tent in the middle of the day. Soon she must have seen a plumpness in her belly and she knew the Lord had fulfilled his promise to her even though she had laughed. After so many years of waiting, after having given up waiting, after so long a time, her feelings must have been bittersweet. If it were possible why did he not do this sooner? If she were truly to bear a son why should it be after so much longing?

Her love for the Lord like her love for Abraham must have been mingled with reproach. But perhaps the first thing she did, even before telling Abraham that God had kept His word, was go to a dark grove on the hill behind their camp and, lying down in the dirt, smelling the sweet dampness that remained there from the previous month's rain, called out to the Lord, "I was wrong to laugh. Forgive me."

She may have been concerned: would the Lord punish her with a child who was lame or blind or missing in mind or limb? Would the Lord punish her for her doubts? Every night before she slept, after the tasks of the day were done, she might have put her hands on her belly, feeling the child move, and said to the Lord, protect him because he is yours, protect him because I meant no harm. When he was born and she saw that he was whole and well she may have wept in relief. She must have felt for the baby in her arms a love that hurt, was closer to pain than joy, so great was it, so large was it.

And her breasts, her ninety-year-old breasts filled with milk for the child. In Genesis 21:7 we read that Sarah said: "Who would have uttered to Abraham 'Sarah is suckling sons!' For I have born a son in his old age."

The rabbis said that when Sarah conceived so did all the barren women on the earth. All those who wished to have a child had a child because of the miracle granted to Sarah.

When Isaac was eight days old he was circumcised by Abraham, and months later when he already smiled at his

mother and held his arms out to all who would hold him his father held a great feast for his weaning.

This story is found in the *Legends of the Jews* by Louis
Ginzberg. Isaac had survived the first months of infancy. God
had not taken him back. All the tribes around were invited to
the feast, and the women were eager to come. Abraham was a
wealthy man with large flocks and stores of grain and boxes of
silver and gold. The women whispered among themselves.
How is it possible that a ninety-year-old woman should have a
child? How could a man as old as Abraham be the child's father? Perhaps they said Abraham was not the true father. Perhaps it had been Abimelech. Or maybe they said Sarah is not
really the baby's mother. She has taken the infant of a slave or
a woman who died and claimed that she gave birth. Sarah
heard the whisperings and she wanted to send all the guests at
the feast home immediately. She wanted to lie down in her tent
with her child and forget the world beyond.

Abraham heard the whisperings and said to Sarah bare your
breasts and suckle all the infants gathered here. Perhaps Sarah
turned her back on her husband and on the assembled crowd.
She would not do such a private thing before all these people.
Again Sarah thought, He will sacrifice my well-being for his
pride, for his wealth, for his safety. Again Abraham ordered
her to nurse all the infants. The crowd was silent, watching.
Many legends embroider this story.

She took her shawl off and she took off her blouse and she
stood tall, and she was a very tall woman, before the crowd. Now
Sarah was without choice. She could not disobey Abraham and
shame him in front of his people. She was his to command.

Silently with no visible expression on her face she opened her shawl, and her full breasts emerged. She took an infant from a woman's arms and gave him milk and then she took another and another. The milk flowed and flowed. The people gazed at her amazed. "It's a trick," someone in the crowd called. Three women came up close to Sarah and touched her breasts, and pulled them to the left and the right, to make sure that they were real, really attached to her chest wall. For three hours Sarah gave milk. The sun crossed the second half of the sky, and still she was giving milk. Then she had her own child brought to her and she suckled him, milk flowing down her breasts, out of the corners of his mouth and all could see. The women were ashamed that they had doubted her motherhood.

This is the second miracle concerning milk for a baby in these stories. This legend echos the tale of Gabriel giving milk from his finger to the infant Abraham.

Perhaps the angel of the Lord who was watching over the feast smiled. It was fine for Sarah to be, at last, the most bountiful mother in the world. This would put an end to the whispers.

Of course it didn't quite put an end to the wicked rumors because the sages reported them in other millennia. It must have been hard for Sarah to endure the doubters and the scoffers at her party. But it was important, important for all time, to make it clear that Sarah and Abraham had been granted an exception from the laws of nature. This is why the sages told the story of the weaning feast. At the very beginning the nation was marked as special and worthy of God's spectacular efforts. This milk legend also demonstrates that the line of the people was uncorrupted and pure. Genesis itself tells us that Abimelech could not have been the father of Sarah's child because his orifices were all closed. Isaac was the son of Abraham and Sarah and all that descended from him would have as their ancestral roots Abraham and Sarah directly back to Noah and Adam. The book of Genesis is the family tree.

Sarah's love for Isaac was not greater because he was so longed for and so delayed. It was as great, as all-consuming as any mother's love for her child. I imagine that all the world was new for her because she was no longer just Sarah, wife of Abraham; now she was Sarah, mother of Isaac. When he laughed her face echoed his joy. She grew pale when he wept from hunger or cold or from the pain of the tooth that was coming but had not yet come and hurried to comfort him.

I imagine that now for Sarah nothing was as it had been before. When a rainbow came she rushed to bring him outside so he could see its splendor. When the cow gave birth she brought him to touch the new calf's silken head. She taught him the names of things, this is a tree and that a pomegranate, and this is the dog who belongs to us, and this is the moon and that is the sun, and so it went, as if she herself were discovering the objects of her world, the people who moved in it, the divisions of time, the wonder of everything. She sung him to sleep with her songs. She woke him to the day with a kiss.

Her plans were laid only to benefit him. It is likely that she now may have been afraid that something would happen to her, a lion tear her to pieces as she sat by the river, a poisonous insect sting her while she walked through the field. If something happened to her, Isaac would be without his mother, and the tragedy of that, of his loss, was near unbearable, just the thought of it, just the fear of it, for him, that is.

*B*ut then Genesis 21:9 tell us that when Isaac was two years old "Sarah saw the son of Hagar the Egyptian, whom she had born to Abraham laughing." Legend tells us she grew afraid for her son and angry at her rival, his mother. She wanted to make sure that Isaac would be the only inheritor of Abraham's wealth and that he would be the son from whom God would make a great nation with as many descendants as the stars in the sky, as the dust in the earth.

Ishmael was the other woman's child. He was Abraham's firstborn, but he was nothing compared to her son. She saw Ishmael with Isaac and determined to remove the mother and the unwanted child from Abraham's sight. She asked Abraham to send Hagar and Ishmael away from their camp. Genesis 21:11 says "the thing seemed evil in Abraham's eyes because of his son." A father of the people could not be so cold of heart as to easily rip out a child from his fold. Perhaps he was not able to erase from his mind Ishmael's first steps, his swim in the deep river on his father's back, his small hands reaching for his father's beard. But God said, "Let it not seem evil in your eyes on account of the lad and on account of your slave girl. Whatever Sarah says to you, listen to her voice for through Isaac shall your seed be acclaimed."

What did Sarah really see to cause her to send Ishmael and

his mother away? The sages tell us many versions of this moment. Did she see just two boys playing? Some say she saw Ishmael throw a rock at Isaac. Some sages defending Sarah's act reported that Ishmael raped virgins. Rabbi Araiah said that Ishmael suggested to Isaac, "Come let us test our mettle in the field" and then Ishmael took up arrows and shot them in Isaac's direction, pretending he was only making sport. Rabbi Akiva says that Sarah saw Ishmael build altars and then catch locusts that he offered to idols. Another sage said that Ishmael had brought a slain lamb to the foot of a local idol, imploring the idol to seduce Abraham into coming into his mother's tent. It was said that he was teaching Isaac to play with his own genitals, and worse, that he was abusing Isaac in a sexual manner. He was said to have mocked those who said Isaac would receive the double portion of the inheritance, saying that he was the first son and all the wealth of Abraham would be his.

If these terrible stories were true then Sarah's virtue would be untouched. Isaac's worth over Ishmael would be established for all time. But these are stories invented by Isaac's descendants who wanted to justify Sarah's behavior and emphasize the worthiness of Isaac's mother. But even Sarah might have wanted the wealth of her husband for her child alone. Even Sarah might have spent years hiding her jealousy, hiding her disappointment in her own barren womb, and then when the moment came, when she herself was a mother and deserving of her husband's loyalty, send her rival away, perhaps to die in the bare hills or to wander in the forest and be eaten by a wild animal. Sarah must have known that alone on the land a human being would be followed by carrion birds circling, and circling, waiting patiently for their meal.

Ishmael must have been a large boy at the time that Abraham sent him away, but with no servants to help him, no sword to protect him, no gold or silver to pay for his food should some caravan come by, he might easily have perished and never been heard from again. In the centuries that followed, some of the sages believed that Sarah wronged herself and God by calling for Hagar's exile. One wrote that her ejection of Hagar explains why Sarah died forty-eight years before her husband. Many rabbis and scholars said all the terrible sorrows that would follow, from exiles to autos-da-fé that befell the Jewish people in the years ahead, were punishment for Sarah's cruelty to Hagar and her son.

Is there a just God or is there not? We long for evil to be punished and good rewarded, but the scales of justice so rarely seem in balance.

When Abraham sent Hagar away with her portion of water and her son on her back he knew that they might not survive.

I imagine that Sarah did not watch them leave. She hid in her tent and played with her baby. In the wild land Ishmael, with the thirst of a young body, soon emptied the sack of water. There was no more. The hot sun beat down and there was no shade, and the mother and son did not have the strength to wander on. Hagar walked away from her child while he was crying out to the Lord to see him there and save him. Hagar settled herself at a distance where she would not have to watch her child grow weaker and his breath become shallow and his hands clutch at the bare ground. Just like Abraham's mother,

Emitali, Hagar could not bear to see her child suffer and die. Hagar's grief was far greater than the joy of triumph was for Sarah. That should never be forgotten.

Some stories were told about Ishmael. They said that he was weakened by an evil eye cast on him by Sarah. That he was sick and feverish and that the water ran out so quickly because his fever dried his skin and gave him a great thirst. With all the terrors of the wild before him, with only one sack of water for the boy and his mother, it probably wasn't necessary to add to Ishmael's catastrophe a fever, an evil eye, a spell. Nature alone would kill the child without help from Sarah. But this story about the fever was invented to protect Abraham's reputation. Would the father of us all have sent his first son out into the wild without enough water to survive? The sages avoid the problem by inventing a feverish Ishmael who drank more water than was expected.

The Lord had promised Abraham that He would make a great nation of Ishmael, and so for the sake of God's plan the boy had to live, and the Lord sent down an angel that spoke to Hagar, saying that God had heard the voice of the child and to look around her. When she did so she saw a well filled with clear blue water and she rushed to it, filling the skin and bringing the cool water to her boy and letting it flow down her own throat.

A sage said that when God let the spring flow to save Ishmael's life His angels protested, "Lord of the Universe, why spare one who will leave your own chosen children to die of thirst?" God answered, "Does he honor me now?" The angels replied, "He still lives in righteousness." God said, "I judge every man as he is now not as he will be."

I can think of many a human being who might better have
been eaten by a famished lion, sparing the world disasters to
come. But then there is something supremely hopeful in the
words of this sage who believed that man should be judged
only on his present acts.

The messenger of God showed Hagar and Ishmael a good
place to live, and the boy became a fine bowman and brought
meat home to his mother, and the two lived on in the wilderness of Paran until his mother took him a wife from the land of
Egypt where she had been born.

That God sent down His angel to protect Hagar and her son
is a sign of God's sometime presence in the lives of women
who are helpless before the cruelty of their masters. The tale
teaches that God intended life for all His peoples. God understood the awesome love a mother holds for her child and welcomed that love as proof of the goodness of His mighty
creation.

Would history have been kinder to the Jewish people if Sarah
had been kinder to her bondswoman and her husband's first
child? It is possible that a division that has caused blood to
soak the ground again and again might have been avoided if
Sarah had not been jealous and if she had been able to love the
child that had not come from her womb but still walked like her
husband, had the black eyes and black hair of her husband.

There is no point in wishing Sarah was someone else. On
the other hand don't forgive her just because she was a woman
who had endured so long without a child. She had sufficient

power to exile her rival and clear Isaac's path to the inheritance of the lands, the animals, and the chests of gold that his father had gathered over the years. And she chose to use it.

The mother of the nation was unable to love a child not her own, a child that was her husband's but not hers. If she had been able to love this child all future history might have been different, tribe might have learned to love tribe. This story tells us how small we are, how limited and conditional our love, how petty we are. Like the lion we defend our own cubs but may kill the others who cross our paths.

Sarah may not have chosen her husband, she may not have determined the route of their travels. She may have been handed over like so many sacks of grain to Pharaoh. She may not have been the center of God's concern, but we see that it is Sarah whose womb fulfills the Lord's promise to Abraham and we see that Sarah's rage against Ishmael sets the stage for endless bloodshed, brother against brother.

Here is another story found in the legends. Years pass, and Abraham, hearing that Ishmael has married, wants to go and visit him in the wilderness of Paran. Sarah forbids him to go. Abraham will not listen to her, his longing for Ishmael is great. Sarah demands a promise from him that he will not dismount from his camel. Abraham finds Ishmael's camp, but Ishmael is not home. His wife does not ask Abraham to dismount, nor does she bring him water or food. She turns her back to him. Abraham tells Ishmael's wife to give her husband a message that an old man has visited and said that his tent peg is broken, to throw it away and get a new one. When Ishmael returns and hears the message he knows his father has come and his wife has not received him with hospitality, so he sends his wife away and gets another. Sometime later Abraham—again not allowed to dismount—visits Ishmael's camp and Ishmael is away on the hunt, but his new wife brings Abraham food and drink and urges him to stay. Abraham sends Ishmael another message: an old man was here and said to tell you your new tent peg is strong and good.

This story tells us that Ishmael did love his father and respected him. It also shows us that Sarah feared her rival long after she had been banished from the camp. Also the story says that Abraham cannot bring himself to disobey his wife. Many men are afraid of their wives.

After the banishment of Hagar and Ishmael the story of Abraham and Sarah comes to its climax, to the part that everyone remembers. Thousands, perhaps millions, of words have been written about it. Over the centuries we find tracts from Jewish scholars who were working in their small studies in the Pale as well as from their fabled academies in Safed, in Vilna, in Lodz. The philosopher Kierkegaard in the endless Swedish night has written on it. So have many Jesuit scholars and Protestant ministers. They all have looked and looked again at this strange story. Painters have illustrated it, musicians have tried to put the words to song. Sermon writers great and small draw a moral from it, maybe the right one, maybe not. The sacrifice of Isaac, called the Akedah, is at the heart of the unfathomable love (is it love?) between man and God.

Sarah is most often ignored in these weighty discussions. And yet it is she who will lose the most if her son is sacrificed according to God's command to Abraham. She does not appear on the stage herself as this story unfolds, but the sages must have known that in ignoring her reactions we deny our own human perspective, which is both male and female, stemming from the love of the mother as well as the love of the father. So as the generations passed they have filled in the tale with her perspective. Unless we recognize Sarah's portion we will always have a partial story, a limited story. What happens to Isaac's mother is part of this tale of obedience to God's command because Abraham was willing not only to sacrifice his son for God but also to destroy the child his wife cherished beyond all else, which must have weighed on his soul heavily.

Perhaps it was at the time of the olive harvest when the oil was being pressed by the servants and the smell of ripe olives was everywhere in the breeze. In the river the fish that had been spawned a month ago were reaching their full size.

Legend says that Satan in the high heavens says to God, "Are you so sure that your favored Abraham will obey you in all matters?" "I am certain of his soul," says God. "Then," says Satan, "see if he will sacrifice his son for you." A sage reports that Satan said to God at the time of the feast for Isaac's weaning, "Look, this Abraham has saved no meat for you. Couldn't he have given you at least a dove or a pigeon?" This is said to begin Satan's urging of God to test the loyalty of Abraham.

This testing of human faith was an old matter. A story came from Babylon years before the tales of Abraham were written down about a man who was the subject of a divine bet and lost everything but still respected the gods. That story was transformed into the book of Job sometime later, but the bones of it had been borrowed from the idol-worshiping neighbors of Mesopotamia. This use of Satan in the book of Genesis is another echo of that ancient story.

Eager to show Satan that Abraham would be loyal to Him under the worst of circumstances, God said to Abraham in Genesis 22:2 "Take, pray, your son, your only one whom you love, Isaac and go forth to the land of Moriah and offer him up as a burnt offering on one of the mountains which I shall show to you." Rashi added this: "Abraham said to him, 'I have two sons.' He said to him, 'Your only one.' Abraham said, 'This one is an only one to his mother and that one is an only to his mother.' God said to Abraham, 'whom you love.' Abraham said, 'I love both of them.' God said to Abraham, 'Isaac.' "

How was Abraham to tell Sarah of this command from his Lord, the one he had devoted his life to defend and worship? The sages say he couldn't. He lied to her and said that he was taking Isaac with him to enter him into a house of study so he would learn the ways of the Lord. The sages, although surely learned, were uncertain of their history, since yeshivas were an invention of another time and another place.

Abraham took Isaac and two servants and brought them to the mountaintop and he took in his hand the cleaver for the sacrifice and he placed the wood for the offering on Isaac's back. A legend reports that Satan tried to divert Abraham: disguised as a shepherd he stopped Abraham as he climbed the mountain, and Satan said to him, "What kind of a God would ask a man to kill his son to please himself? This God does not deserve your love." Abraham did not turn back. He was not tempted to swerve away from the service of the Lord, who had demanded this terrible thing from him. In this he was as firm as the mountain itself, rooted in his love of God like the rocks of the mountain into the soil of the land. A little farther up the path Satan tried again. He approached Isaac and told him that his hours of life were short. "Run," he said to him. "Don't let your father do this thing that he will regret all his days. You must live for your mother. She will die if she hears that you have been offered on the altar." Isaac said, "I will gladly die if that is what the Lord has asked of me."

In these tales Satan tries to prove Abraham unworthy with the very arguments that we would use to stop this dreadful plan.

Here is another story. Isaac said to his father as they approached the mountaintop, "When you tell mother that I am dead make sure she is not on a high place, not standing on a roof or high above a river, for she will throw herself down. She will not want to live anymore." The thing that God demanded of Abraham was hard.

On the third day, Abraham bound Isaac on the altar. According to Rabbi Yohanan and Rabbi Yose Ben Zimra this was done on the third day so the world would not say God deranged Abraham so that he cut his son's throat. If he had rushed to obey this might seem true. Abraham wanted it to be clear that his was not an act of madness but of obedience to the

Lord. It is said that Isaac said to his father, "Hurry do the will of your maker. Burn me into a fine ash and then take the ash to my mother—say to her—'This is my son, whom his father has slaughtered.'"

And what of Sarah, waiting for her husband and son to return? She is accustomed to waiting for the men to return from the fields, from the harvest, from visits to the town where they bring the animals and the grains and sell them for silver bars and rugs woven in far-off cities. But this time she is eager for the return of her husband and son. There was something in the abruptness of Abraham's words when he left, the way he turned his head away from her face, the way he touched her arm, that disturbed her.

She decided to take the path to Hebron and wait for him there under the great elms at Mamre. There is a legend that Satan found her there and disguised himself as Isaac. There was dirt on his clothes and a long scratch down his face that had come from the wood on which he had been tied. His eyes were red from tears. "Mother," he said, "Father took me to a mountain and tied me to a pile of wood and he took out his knife and would have cut my throat as an offering to God if a ram had not appeared and the angels told him to give God the ram instead of me."

There is another version of this part of the story. Satan comes to Sarah and tells her that Abraham has bound her son on the altar and sacrificed him to his God. Sarah hears these words and assumes that Isaac is dead.

The story continues according to the modern biblical scholar Aviva Zoren Gornberg as Sarah cries out. Her cry was the same as the sound that the shofar makes, a wail, a complaint, a great broken sound. Her wail contained her fury at Abraham for following such a command. What man would offer his own son as a sacrifice? She cried again, and this time the sound was like that of an animal bleating in pain, it contained the fury she felt at the Lord, whom she had served all her life and done as He asked and moved when He asked her to move and tried in all ways to be worthy of His care and believed in Him when all around had idols whom they worshiped, idols who would not have asked for the death of her child, her only child.

She cried again in despair because she knew then that the generations to follow could not depend on the hand of the Lord to save them from the evils He himself would design. She cried because she could no longer believe that the good would be rewarded and the bad punished. She saw her own life as built on a rock of feathers. She saw the great world as a swirl of darkness moving nowhere, toward no one, chaos returned, a hole, an abyss. That was what she knew, and from that abyss her cry rose.

The sages say that some who heard her wail went deaf, others trembled in their limbs ever after. It was said that Sarah's cry caused a man to lose his sight and another was never able to walk again.

Isaac lived, but what did that matter, her husband was willing to kill her child for the God who had asked for his death as if he were an antelope, a goat, a calf. Instantly then Sarah died, there at Kiriath-Arba. Her soul left her body.

She was 127 years old.

The sages said that when she died at 127 she was as free of sin at 100 as she was at 20 and as beautiful at 20 as she had been at 7. It was important to the commentators on the story that Sarah be extraordinary, and while this particular effort with the numbered years of her life seems strained, the intention was to praise her unusual moral and physical virtue and so to prove her worthy of the miracle of birth that was granted her so late in life.

Legend tell us that there was a cloud above Sarah's tent while she lived. This cloud was the sign of the divine presence over her home. When she died the cloud disappeared. Some say it was a light that was extinguished with her death.

Would she have been comforted if she knew that after the ram lay on the wood, his throat slit, his blood seeping over the logs, the smoke of the fire curling upward, the Lord had promised Abraham again that He would bless him and multiply his seed as the stars in the heaven and as the sand on the shore of the sea? Would it have mattered to her that He said, "Your seed shall take hold of its enemies' gate"? And that, "All the nations of the earth will be blessed through your seed because you have listened to my voice"?

This is the first time that Abraham has been promised military victory over his foes, but this promise contains the information that there would be foes, there would be strife, ahead lay the death of a multitude of young men whose mothers would weep.

The Lord had promised this increase of Abraham's seed before. Shouldn't the Lord need to make only one promise if he intended to keep it?

And what of the ram whose miraculous appearance saved Isaac's life? Rabbi Eliezer said, "The Ram came from the mountains where he had been grazing." R. Joshua differed, saying, "An angel brought him from the Garden of Eden where he had been grazing beneath the tree of life and drinking the waters that passed under it." He said, "The Ram had been placed in the Garden during twilight at the end of the six days of creation." In Zechariah 9:4 it says, "The ram was entangled in the brush and thrashed and turned several times. The Holy One said, so shall your children be trapped in kingdoms from Babylon to Media from Media to Greece, from Greece to Edom. In the end they will be redeemed at the sound of the horn of this ram." None of this would likely have comforted Sarah.

Word of Sarah's death came to Abraham at Beersheva, and he came immediately to Hebron to mourn his wife. In Hebron there was a cave that he had found when the three angels had visited him at Mamre when he ran to slaughter a calf for them. He had followed the calf into the dark passage of a deep cave. Its darkness, its dampness, its boulders, large and small, determined his path. After a while he saw a light ahead and there, according to legend, he saw Adam and Eve stretched out on a rock, holding hands like innocent children. Then the light faded and he saw them no longer and he turned and walked back to the surface of the earth.

He spoke to the Hittites, whose land he was standing on. He asked them to grant him this land as a burial place, and they called him a prince of the Lord. Ephron son of Zohar sold to him, for the exorbitant price of four hundred shekels, the field at Machpelah and with it the cave in the field, the very cave where Abraham had seen the first man and the first woman.

In the *Babylonian Tractate* Rabbi Alexandre said, "The world becomes darkened for a man whose wife dies in his lifetime. The light is dark in his tent and the lamp above him is put out." Rabbi Yose B. Hanina said, "His strong steps are shortened."

Rabbi Samuel. b. Naham said, "for everything there is a substitute except for the wife of one's youth."

Nevertheless Abraham married again. His second wife's name was Keturah, and this wife had six sons who became six nations. There is a legend that this second wife was actually Hagar whom he had always loved along with Sarah.

In the book of Genesis Abram's life was with Sarai above all others. Her life was only with him. Deep in the cave where the two lie together for all eternity, there is no one else, they belong to each other. Almost.

Sarah was the first wife, the mother of Isaac, but life continues in a pedestrian way, urges rise, children are born, accidents happen, one travels from here to there, other stories wait their turn. Sarah was virtuous. Her virtue was not born of fear, born of convention, born of cowardice. Hers was a virtue of being. Her breath was the same as the breath of her husband. The animals went into the ark by twos. Adam had Eve. Noah had his wife. A Man and a Woman live in God's sight together. This is virtue in a way. It is custom in a way. It is habit as well as a necessary matter to assure that the children live to have children of their own. Marriage keeps the world from falling into chaos. For Sarai and Abram it seems to be the reason for their strength, the reason for their worthiness. Yes, Abram also had Hagar, and custom would have allowed him other wives and many concubines, but Abraham is buried with Sarah. They come to us in text and commentary together, man and wife.

*S*arah's value lies not in her moral attributes, which are simply human, imperfect in fact. Her place in the tale is not because of her magical skills, her special closeness to God, her invention of a new mode of thought. We do not honor her as we do other heroines because of her courage in war, her devotion to the poor or the sick. She did not save the people in a time of danger, like Judith or Esther, or become a great judge like Deborah. She did not control the events around her. Her place of honor is assured because of the recognizable human dimensions of her life, a life like that of the women around her, the women who came before her, the women who would follow her. Her honor lies in her devotion to the one true God whom she served always as best she could.

She endured the disappointment of her infertility. She endured the hardships that came to her people. She experienced jealousy and love. She felt the sting of humiliation. She was proud and sometimes ungenerous. As are we all.

She is the mother of the nation. She is not a goddess who can intervene in human life. She was beautiful but she caused no calamity like Helen of Troy. While a miracle occurred that permitted her to give birth at age ninety this miracle was surely a bittersweet gift and increased our respect for God, rather than our awe of Sarah.

Nevertheless we are proud of her. She belongs to us. Dimly we see her through the text. We hear her laugh at the pronouncement of God's messengers. We see her anger at Hagar and Ishmael. We know that she was not the last female to nearly lose everything as man and God tested each other down the ages.

At the beginning there was Sarah, who was Abraham's wife and Isaac's mother. Her story tells us of drought and exile, near rape, envy, infertility, warfare. She was a woman with a role to play in God's plan for humanity. Through her womb, through the miracle of her conception at the age of ninety, the nation began its long journey toward what end, for what purpose, we do not yet know. But many believe that at the end redemption waits. The world will be repaired and the gates of Eden opened to all.

And her son Isaac loved her.

Rebekah

How was it? Perhaps like this: the men were in the fields harvesting the grapes and the olives, filling sacks with green fruits that hung ripe and heavy on the branches. Abraham sat in the front of his tent and watched the donkeys moving up and down the nearby hill. His bones ached. His arms, which had always been able to carry two calves at a time, were now veined and bony. His beard was silver, his hair had turned white as milk, and the skin on his face was translucent. He could not stand without help from his second wife, Keturah, or one of the six sons he had given her. A sage has said that Abraham only began to feel old after the death of Sarah.

Abraham knew that his final days had come. He said to his servant Eliezer, who ruled over all things that concerned his master, in Genesis 24:3, "You shall not take a wife for my son from the daughters of the Canaanites in whose midst I dwell, but to my land, and to my birthplace, you shall go, and you shall take a wife for my son, for Isaac." Abraham wanted Eliezer to go to the land of Ur, in Haran, where his brother's people lived.

Eliezer set out with, legend tells us, a dozen men to protect him, a supply of food for many days, and water in the event that no well was available. He also brought goats and sheep, donkeys, and ten camels with their saddlebags filled with treasures for the bride whom he hoped to find for Isaac in the distant country from which his master had come. As he rode away, Eliezer's camel was followed by other camels stretching along the horizon's edge. Eliezer prayed to the one true God to lead him. He moved slowly through the high grasses. He was a faithful servant and had sworn an oath that he would bring back a bride from Abraham's people. He had placed his hand under Abraham's genitals and made a promise to do this thing. This way of swearing an oath was a reminder of the act of circumcision, which marked the covenant between Abraham and God. That is the way that oaths were made in that part of the world, in those distant days. Abraham told him he would be free of his oath if the girl he chose refused to return with him. Eliezer had also promised never to take Isaac out of the land that the Lord had granted to Abraham and his descendants.

In the land of Canaan there were many peoples, in the towns and in the rolling hills, near the lakes, near the sea, that worshiped El and Asharah. They sacrificed to their gods with the entrails of goats and sheep and calves and perhaps with the blood of little children offered to Baal, god of war, and to Anat and Astante, his wives. Some prayed to Shamash, the sun god, and some prayed to Reshop, friend of warriors, or to Huron, who was said to protect the souls of the dead. Some kept small idols in their tents, teraphim that would accept the prayers of a woman with a sick child, or a man whose herds were diminishing because of the wolves.

It was only Abraham and his followers that worshiped an invisible God, one God, whose name was Eloheim, or perhaps He bore another name so awesome it would never be pronounced. All around Abraham the tribes he traded with, the tribes who tried to steal his wells, the tribes he made his allies and those he fought, all of them believed that chaos ruled in the heavens, that gods fought with one another, that man in his helplessness could only offer sacrifices and hope that his life would be spared and his riches increase, that sickness not befall him, that accidents not cripple, that the darkness not hide the approaching steps of the enemy.

All the gods were needed because death and loss were as near as the fingers on the ends of a man's hand.

A sage of another time, Martin Buber, said, "The world is like the blade of a knife, the netherworld is above and the netherworld is below."

But Abraham did not want an idol worshipper to marry his son. He did not want to mix his line with the line of his neighbors who had turned deaf when he told them that there was only one God and all the others were inventions of the feverish human mind. God had given great promises to Abraham's progeny, and He had said that Isaac would be the instrument of His will. Rabbenu Nissim had attributed Abraham's rejection of a Canaanite wife to the moral depravity of that tribe. They were said to have sexual orgies twice a year in which everyone had sex with one another to the sound of beating drums. They were said to have feasts at their temples in which the men wore women's clothes. They were said to kill their own children and drink their blood.

Canaanite women were allowed to have sex with many partners before marriage, whereas the Hebrews insisted on virginity in their brides. The families where authority ran through the blood of the mother did not make an issue of virginity, but those where power rested with the male did. But Isaac was innocent and pure and Abraham wanted a virginal wife for his son.

It was possible that the Canaanites were no worse than other people and were slandered in the same manner that the citizens of Lvov said terrible things about the sanitary habits of the citizens of Vilna. If instead of this dislike of the Canaannites Abraham had formed deep friendships with them and allowed his son to marry one of their daughters everything that followed would have changed. But there would have been no peoples to pray to the one God, the one God who would present to mankind a moral life, a good life, an ideal of peace and justice.

What if Isaac had been tempted away from God by his Canaanite wife? What then would have become of the world? But of course he didn't have a Canaanite wife.

There is a legend that when Abraham asked Eliezer to find a wife for Isaac, Eliezer offered his own daughter. Abraham replied, "You, Eliezer are a bondman, Isaac is free born: the cursed may not unite with the blessed." This is not a story that speaks well of Abraham's compassion. But it does make clear to all future readers that Abraham and his descendants were free people, who followed God willingly.

*A*braham's servant traveled to Paddan-aram in Haran. Some Hasidic masters said that this journey only took a bare minute or two and that the group was instantly transported by a heavenly wind and arrived in Paddan-aram a bare second after they started. But this magic trip was not the way God usually revealed His hand in human affairs. Sorcerers and witches may have traveled in the folds of a magical wind but God's people moved across the hills, one foot at a time, only as fast as the animals could carry them, with need of rest and water and food. It was far more likely that the journey took Eliezer more than a few months. He pitched his camp on the land, and sometimes it rained and sometimes he could find little water, and perhaps the men who were with him quarreled. When at last he arrived at his destination it was nearing eventide. He waited at the great well outside the encampment. He made the camels kneel down. He prayed to God.

Genesis 24:13 says, "Here I am poised by the spring of water and the daughters of the men of the town are coming out to draw water. Let it be that the young woman whom I say, 'Pray, tip down your jug that I may drink' if she says, 'Drink and your camels, too, I shall water,' she it is whom you have marked for your servant, for Isaac."

Over a slope of the hill he saw several young women approaching, their pitchers held on their shoulders. They may have called to one another in greeting.

Maybe it was like this: Rebekah approached alone. On her right shoulder she held a large clay pitcher. Dust from the path covered her sandals. A few beads of perspiration were running down her face. Her skin was smooth and browned by the sun. Her face was pleasing, and her black wide eyes seemed to notice everything and approve of all they saw, including the stranger at the well who was staring at her. She held the pitcher with one arm, as if it were no more than a loaf of bread. She walked with determination, a steady walk, unafraid. Her dark hair had slipped out from its binding, and easily she pushed it back away from her eyes. She paused as she approached the rim of the well. The light behind her was fading. The evening star would within the hour pull up over the horizon's edge. Her beauty could not be questioned.

She was a virgin.

She was dressed in the way that maidens of the time dressed.

Rebekah's birth is announced in Genesis 22. She was the granddaughter of Abraham's brother Nahor and his wife Milcah. Her father was Bethuel and her brother was Laban. Abraham's acceptance of the one God must surely have been part of the family's belief. Perhaps the family of Bethuel was not as pure in their conviction as Abraham, but surely they had joined his way of thinking, his opposition to idol worship. Rebekah is the only woman in all the pages of the Testament whose birth is announced. Among the begats and begats of a long line of fathers and sons here is the sole woman worthy of record, or so it seems. It is said by the sages that Rebekah's birth and future betrothal to Isaac had been announced to

Abraham when he was on Mount Moriah, right after he had sacrificed the ram instead of his son. Many sages puzzled over the numbers involved. If Rebekah was born when Abraham climbed the mountain then she would have been three years old when Eliezer found her by the well. But the numbers and the ages are not the point. What the sages wanted to say was that Rebekah was intended from birth for Isaac and this marriage was God's design.

Perhaps the day had been like any other day. She woke early and folded away the bed covers. She opened the flaps to her tent, the one she shared with her little cousins, and she went to the stream and washed herself. There was in her young body a certain restlessness. She saw the young girls playing a game up on the dirt mound before the sheep pen. For a moment she wanted to join them, to run and chase the stone they were passing one to another. But she knew she was not a child anymore. She stood tall and stretched her arms high, as if she were reaching for a cloud. She may have felt the morning sun on her back, not yet hot, but soothing, like a song you sing to a baby.

This day would be the beginning of her own story, separate from her brother's, separate from the family and the place she had known all her life. Soon she would become something else, soon her future would be revealed. Her fate was in God's hands. She smiled at her reflection in the water. She must have trusted in his plan for her. She was not shy nor was she forward. She had no need.

Perhaps her brother Laban no longer looked at her face. He turned his head sideways when she entered his tent. She understood this was right. He was right to do so.

She may have thanked God for the morning, for the sun, which was now white in the sky. She may have thanked God for all the gentle and good things she knew. She may have remembered her grandfather's death, the year the sickness fell on the sheep, the hunger that she had known then, but still she gave thanks. "Whatever you ask of me, I will do," she may have said aloud. Perhaps she had been saying these same words since she was old enough to understand. They would have brought her peace.

As the day drew toward its end she went down to the well. The slope was very steep. Rebekah took her pitcher off her shoulder and filled it to the brim. She placed it back on her shoulder and walked steadily, her weight carefully balanced, her legs bent slightly. A strange man spoke to her when she arrived at the top. Genesis 24 says, "Pray let me sip a bit of water from your jug." And she lowered the pitcher into her hands and tipped it over for him and she said, "Drink my Lord." She let him drink. Then she said, "For your camels too, I shall draw water until they drink their fill." And so she went down the many steps again to the well and up again and emptied the water into the trough and then again and again, for the camels had come a long way and were very thirsty and there were many of them and her pitcher was only as large as her shoulder could bear. Perhaps her legs grew tired before she had brought enough water for more than half the beasts, but she did not stop. She knew the animals needed the water. She had promised and so she continued, breathing now heavily, spilling some of the water on the way up. She did not stop until the last camel had lifted his head from the trough in contentment.

Ovadiah Seforno, the sixteenth-century Italian scholar, says that Rebekah's haste to fill her pitcher for the visitor and his beasts reveals how important it was to her that hospitality be offered and the stranger be comforted. Another sage writes that, like Abraham, his future daughter-in-law "hurried" to satisfy the needs of a stranger, and the word *hurried* is used on both occasions to indicate how eagerly both hearts complied with the perceived need of the other. To give charity to the poor, to stop a bandit from robbing a helpless widow, to live an upright life, without stealing from others or harming their children or committing acts of sexual violation, these were the tests of virtue that mattered in the world, but when Abraham was on earth the one true test was how you treated a stranger because the temptation to violate the stranger was strong. The knowledge that we are all human and in need of one another was the great rock of wisdom at the time.

Hospitality was the golden rule, hospitality was the test, the test that the people of Sodom and Gomorrah had failed, and Abraham had passed. Rebekah with her kind heart and her willing hands and her strong arms was God's choice for His people. Also she was closely related to Abraham, and the story of Genesis is a story of the generations bound together by blood as well as echoes in the story, repetitions and variations.

The legends tell another tale. In this one Eliezer watched as the water in the well rose up to Rebekah so she didn't need to go down the steps to fill her pitcher. The water rose to Rebekah's feet because the Angel Michael recognized her kindness to the stranger. But it is even more remarkable to think of the young woman again and again filling her pitcher for the camels of a stranger.

A sage noted that Rebekah running up and down the steep sides of the well reminds us of an Homeric act, such as the cleaning of the Aegean stables, a performance of extraordinary physical strength. However, the emphasis in the Rebekah story here is not on her athletic capacity but on her moral quality.

Eliezer pulled from one of his saddlebags a heavy gold nose ring, and two bracelets for Rebekah's arms, and in addition he gave her ten gold shekels in weight. He asked her whose daughter she was and he asked her if there was room in her father's house for his men and himself and a place for his animals. And she said to him, Genesis 24:23, " 'I am the daughter of Bethuel, the son of Milcah whom she bore to Nahor.' And she said to him, 'We have abundance of bran and feed as well and room to spend the night.' " Eliezer bowed down to the Lord, God of my master Abraham and thanked him for his kindness, the kindness that had led him to the house of Abraham's kinsmen. Rashi says that her kindness and courtesy extended so far that she answered his questions in the order in which they were asked.

Did Rebekah understand these gifts as a bridal offer? She must have understood that this ordinary matter of watering animals, giving a man a drink from her pitcher, had won the heart of the stranger. She herself had likely never before owned a nose ring, or a gold shekel, or a bracelet for her arm. She must have been concerned: was it all right to accept these gifts from a stranger, had she done something wrong in inviting him home, would her father and brother be angry with her? The peace that she had felt that morning might now have deserted her. Was she in danger? Or was this good fortune? Perhaps she forgot her pitcher by the well. She ran back to her house and placed all the offerings on a rug before her mother's household and told all that had happened.

Was this an end or a beginning—were paths opening or were they closing? She would have shown her family no tears. She was calm before them, although the muscles of her legs might have been trembling. Her brother Laban would not have reassured her. He carefully examined the gifts she had received and took them from her and then he went off to see the stranger at the spring. Perhaps Rebekah went to her tent and changed her clothes. She might have tied her red sash around her waist. Her nurse Deborah might have brushed her hair. She went back and sat by her mother's side.

Laban ran to the well. Genesis 24:31 says, "Come in, blessed of the Lord, why should you stand outside when I have readied the house and a place for the camels." He took Eliezer and his fellow servants to Bethuel's house, where the servants took off the saddles and the bags that had weighed the camels down. Water must have been brought for the travelers to wash their weary feet. Platters of food were placed before them. But Eliezer said, in Genesis 24:33, "I will not eat until I have spoken my word. I am Abraham's servant. The Lord has blessed my master abundantly and he has grown great. He has given him sheep and cattle and silver and gold and male and female slaves and camels and donkeys." Eliezer told his story to Laban. He was seeking a bride for the son of his master Abraham and had asked God for a sign and had received it. Rebekah was certainly the maiden he was sent to bring to Abraham's son Isaac. He told them of Abraham's love for the family he had left behind in Paddan-aram. Then he said, in Genesis 24:49, "And so if you are going to act with steadfast kindness toward my master tell me, and if not tell me, that I may turn elsewhere."

There is no record of Laban inquiring, What kind of a man is this you are offering my sister? Is his word good? Is his manner gentle toward women or is he a brute, a slayer of wild things? Does he care about the men who till his field? Does he hold each life dear? Perhaps Laban asked about the size of the flock, the numbers of camels, the piles of grain at harvesttime. Then he said that the matter seems to have come from God and so must be.

Rebekah waited in her mother's tent. She did not hear the questions or the answers. Perhaps a bondswoman who had been waiting to serve the men their meal ran to Rebekah's place and told the womenfolk that there was talk of marriage to a man who lived far away in Canaan.

The bondswoman may have promised to come again to the women to let them know what was happening as soon as it was clear, as soon as something had been determined.

Rebekah and her mother could do nothing but wait for the men to decide between them if this was to be or not. Perhaps Rebekah could not keep her fingers still. Perhaps they twisted and turned, smoothed and ruffled her robe, turned her belt forward and backward. She may have wanted to run like a young girl in circles around the room.

What she would not have wanted was to marry a man who would be set upon by his neighbors and she carried off as a slave. She would not have wanted to be hungry or have her children grow frail from lack of grain or milk. She would not have wanted to be among people who cavorted in the night around the fire in a way that God could not approve. What she must have feared was a place where there would be no food, no crops, no laughter in the fields.

Who was she? She was strong, we know from her watering of the camels. She was kind and respectful, we know from her initial conversation with Eliezar. We can assume that she loved the one true God, whom she must have learned about from her family. She was intelligent, as we know from how later she laid plans to give the nation of Abraham its proper founder. She was brave, as we know from her willingness to leave her mother's side and journey far away to an unknown future.

Rebekah's mother had been summoned into the room where the men now sat. Rebekah's mother must have been told that an agreement had been reached. She saw that Eliezer had brought out of his bags beautiful garments for Rebekah and gold bars that were gifts for her parents. Without Rebekah's consent or the consent of her mother it had been arranged.

A feast was prepared.

Rebekah was fourteen years old, although some commentators say she was twenty.

There is a legend that the marriage was not agreed upon so easily at all. They say that Laban saw Rebekah's gold nose ring and her bracelets and had decided to rob Eliezer of all he had. He and his men went to the well with that intention, but then he saw how large and strong Eliezer was and how many men he had with him, and he decided instead to invite him home for a feast. After Eliezer had stated his mission, Laban poisoned the food brought before Eliezer. Eliezer put a piece of poisoned lamb into a folded portion of bread and brought it to his mouth. But the Angel Gabriel, invisible to the human eye, but with wings folded behind him, with long arms and flowing hair and eyes that let out their own sharp light, entered the room and pushed Eliezer in the back so he dropped the bread and the lamb. As he reached for another piece the angel exchanged Eliezer's plate with that of Bethuel. Bethuel, Rebekah's father, took a small piece of cooked lamb and called out in pain and died right there. The son must have been appalled at what he had done. The mother would have wept. Rebekah would have wept for her father.

This—which might have happened but might not—would explain why in Genesis Bethuel is not the one to give Rebekah to Eliezer. Some sages were upset by this legend, not wanting to believe that such wickedness could have existed in Rebekah's family. The story may have been invented to discredit Laban because of his later behavior, but fair is fair. It was unlikely that Bethuel had been murdered and far more likely that he had died suddenly. He was old. He was weak. All mysteries are not murder mysteries.

However there is another reason why the author of the tales needed to remove Bethuel from the story. It was said that in those days among the peoples of the area it was the right of the father of the bride to deflower her on her wedding night. The Hebrew custom demanded virginity from the bride, and

Rebekah would have been disqualified as a mother of the nation had her virginity been taken by her father or another. Conveniently, in Genesis 24, Bethuel just disappeared from the story, and in legend he was murdered in the nick of time. In many Middle Eastern countries the bride's maidenhead is still tested on her wedding night by the bridegroom's finger. Here is another version of the same story. "It was said that Bethuel was the King of Haran and had claimed the sole right to deflower the brides of his people and when Rebekah became nubile, the princes of the land gathered around, saying: 'unless Bethuel now treats his own daughter as he has treated ours we shall kill them both.'" For the sake of the tale, for the sake of the pure lineage of the people, Bethuel had to disappear and he did.

The servant of the father of the faraway husband-to-be told her brother and mother how important it was that he find a woman from his master's family. He told her brother and father that Rebekah was God's choice. Laban nodded and said the right words. Her mother may have bowed her head in agreement although there may have been small tears at the corners of her eyes. She must have known this would happen one day. The child at her breast would be given in marriage and taken off to another place. It is not a death, Rebekah's mother would have reminded herself. It is not an end but a beginning.

In the morning Eliezer said (Genesis 24:55), "'Send me off, that I may go to my master.' And her brother and her mother said, 'Let the young woman stay with us ten days or so, then she may go.'" But Eliezer insisted that Rebekah be given to him immediately. The sages say he did not want Laban to change his mind, to demand more treasure than he could supply, to hold the girl back from him. Genesis 24:58 says, "And they called Rebekah and said to her, 'Will you go with this man?' And she said, 'I will.' "

The sages also say that Eliezer did not trust Laban not to murder him and take the dowry for himself. Some of the sages say that the family wanted Rebekah to remain to mourn for her father. These are the stories that were told across the towns and villages of another time. Genesis itself just tells us that Laban is the one who sent Rebekah off.

Perhaps Rebekah went to her nurse, who is called Deborah by some of the storytellers, although not named in Genesis. Together they may have folded her things. Rebekah may have piled her pillows together and Deborah wrapped them with string.

What we know of Rebekah from all this is that she was a girl with great courage and that she herself was the answer to Eliezer's prayer to God so that God himself has selected her to be one of the mothers of the people. It was surely her goodness of soul that guided His choice. It was surely the radiance of her spirit and her willingness to follow where her fate would lead that determined God's choice of this particular young woman. Yes, her bloodlines were right, but there were others who might also have qualified, cousins perhaps. But she was clearly chosen because of her fine spirit, kindness, strength, directness, and her loyalty to the one true God.

The sun was already strong as Eliezer stood by his camels ready for departure. Rebekah and her women came to him, and the men loaded the packages into the bags and onto the kneeling beasts who turned their heads to stare. Laban and his men were there. Laban said to Rebekah, Genesis 24:60:

> *"Our sister, become hence myriads teeming,*
> *may your seed take hold of the gate of its foes."*

*S*ome sages say that this poem was muttered and the tone was sarcastic because Laban envied her for the good fortune she had found.

No one tells us of Rebekah's mother's last words to her daughter. She must have been shadowed by thoughts of her child all the rest of her days. The pain of childbirth was just the beginning of God's punishment for Eve's sin. The pain that comes with the loss of a child is far worse and never fades. Rebekah must have remembered her mother each day and each night. Ever after, we carry with us a yearning for the love we knew in childhood.

The camels rose and headed west, away from the rising sun. Perhaps Rebekah was pitched forward and then back and she held tightly to the saddle. The motion of the moving camel must soon have calmed her. Then perhaps her home grew small in the distance and she stopped looking back. She looked ahead of her at the brush. She saw the flies buzzing about the ears of the camel. This was to be the only journey of her life. She would be transplanted to the Canaanite land, a stranger from far away, but she came from Abraham's family. She was the one who would bring the family back together again. At night she must have slept an untroubled sleep, without remembering her dreams. Perhaps sometimes she walked alone, swinging her arms out at her sides. She must have been covered with dust. She must have splashed in the river where they stopped.

She must have wondered about her husband-to-be. She must have wondered if he was strong or brave. Her bondswomen may have heard from the men in the camp that their new master had survived a terrible ordeal. The sages said of Isaac that he was gentle and abhorred violence. They said that he was in mourning for his mother a very long time. Perhaps he refused to stray far from his mother's tent.

Isaac had settled near Beer Lahai Roi. He had been given all his father's wealth. The land was rich and ample for the feeding of his flocks and the growing of grain and the tending of the olive trees. But he must have been alone with his thoughts, alone with his grief for his mother. The sages say that he never recovered from his ordeal on the mountaintop. It was likely that every morning and every evening he thanked God for his life, but he could no more have understood God's request nor forgiven his father for following it than can the thousands of scholars and philosophers who have considered the sacrifice in the years that followed. Perhaps after he came down from the mountain he never assumed that the morning would find him alive. He must have been a man who believed that permission for him to live could be revoked at any moment.

This marriage was God's wish. Rebekah would not have doubted that.

I imagine that they crossed the river slowly, donkeys and camels, saddlebags filled with baskets of dates and figs. Rebekah must have seen the stars changing positions in the night sky as she made her way from her first home to her last home.

They must have traveled through wide green pasturelands and up the hills into the edge of the high forest and over the rocks and through the swarms of flies and the rustling of rodents.

*T*he sages tell us that at sunset many days later they reached the well of Lahai Roi, where God had once comforted Hagar. Genesis 24:62 says, "Issaac had come from the approach to Beer-laha-roi as he was dwelling in the Negeb region." Across the field Rebekah saw a man walking. Perhaps the sun was behind him, turning him into a silhouette. In Genesis 24:65, she said, "'Who is that man walking through the field toward us?' And the servant said, 'He is my master.'" With that Rebekah pulled her camel to a halt. She slid off her saddle and felt the firm earth beneath her feet. Rashi says, "She saw him majestic and she was dumbfounded in his presence." Perhaps she also sees that he is alone and has need of her kindness. She veiled herself. This was right.

When Penelope, who came to Ithaca to marry Odysseus, first saw her husband-to-be, she too veiled herself. At that time, historians of the Middle East think, women were veiled as brides but not as they walked about the world, as has become the custom now in many countries. Freud would tell us that the veil, which must be lifted to see the face, is like the hymen that protects the gate of pleasure. The face that after marriage must, as custom still bids, be hidden from the world is the symbolic substitution for the site of reproduction, the most private and sacred possession of a woman and the man who is her husband.

Penelope too was said to be the first woman to have made a marriage that brought her to her husband's people.

Isaac must have walked forward. He must have seen the camels and his father's servant. Perhaps he reached for her hand. Perhaps she let him take it, his fingers warm around hers.

Behind the couple came Rebekah's nurse, Deborah, and then the bondswomen. Eliezer and his servants must have stood watching. The moon, a new sliver of a moon, a tiny crescent of light, may have appeared. A hornet might have passed by Rebekah's veiled face. She brushed it away.

Her eyes must have looked at Isaac without fear or pity or any sign of regret.

Perhaps a servant brought them food and drink. And then when the night was very dark and the moon high in the sky they lay down together.

Genesis 24:67: "And Isaac brought her into the tent of Sarah his mother and took Rebekah as a wife. And he loved her, and Isaac was consoled after his mother's death."

The sages say that when Rebekah arrived, the warm light that had floated above Sarah's tent returned. Some sages say it was a cloud containing the divine spirit that had left the tent when Sarah died but that it returned when Rebekah entered.

Perhaps all around the inside of the tent a soft light seemed to glow. It was not the light of moon or star; it was an illumination fired by the heat of the new bond, a bond between man and woman, man and wife, made of human sweat and mixed with tears of loss, loss of mother, loss of father, loss of childhood, loss of innocence. It was the light of soul touching soul that filled the tent. Or it may have been God's presence, there in the tent.

Isaac may have given thanks to God even though this was the same God, the only God, who had asked his father to bring him to Mount Moriah and slit his throat with the same long knife that had on other days put an end to so many calves and so many sheep.

There is another legend about this meeting between Rebekah and Isaac. On the way down from the peak of Mount Moriah Abraham and Isaac lost sight of each other in a great fog. Then Isaac was taken up to Paradise, lifted in the arms of the Angel Gabriel, where all of God's minions brought him gifts that might heal his wounded soul after his near sacrifice on the mountain. He stayed in Paradise three years, learning to love and trust again, and then he was released back onto earth just as Eliezer with Rebekah behind him approached Isaac's home. Rebekah looked across the field and saw Isaac walking on his hands. She was startled. "Who is that?" she said to Eliezer. "That is a man who was dead but will soon right himself and return to the living," said Eliezer. Just at that moment Isaac saw Rebekah, and he turned himself around so his feet were pressing into the earth and his hands were free to reach for her. Perhaps his hands were covered with dirt, so an angel blew away the dirt leaving his palms white and soft so he would not stain his bride-to-be.

For many centuries people believed that the dead walked on their hands when they visit earth.

There is a third legend found in Robert Graves and Raphael

Patai's book, *Hebrew Myths,* about Rebekah's arrival in Canaan at Isaac's camp. In this one she saw Isaac walking on his hands as the dead do and she took fright and fell off her camel and was hurt by the branch of a bush. Abraham was there in the welcoming party when Eliezer arrived with the bride he had brought for Isaac. Abraham said to his son, "Take this woman into your tent and finger her to see whether she is still a virgin after this long journey in Eliezer's company."

Isaac did as his father told him. He touched her there and saw that her maidenhead was broken. He was very angry. She must be immediately returned to her brother's house. Rebekah swore by the living God that no man had touched her. Isaac was dragging her to his father without saying a word to her when he caught sight of her lovely face and the tears that were running down it. He asked her, "How has this happened? How could this be?" Rebekah told him that she had been frightened by his appearance and fallen off her camel and a branch had pierced her between her thighs. She took Isaac to the place where she had fallen, and there on the branch were drops of her virginal blood. Isaac then believed her.

Meanwhile Eliezer had been placed under guard and was about to be executed because Abraham was convinced that he had raped Rebekah. Before this could happen God took Eliezer into Paradise alive, and so in a manner of speaking there is a happy end to this version of the tale.

The Rambam said that when Isaac saw Rebekah he went to plant trees. The land was hospitable to trees and trees bore fruit and flowers, but you claim the land by planting on it. A tree is not put in the ground for the pleasure of the planter but

is intended as a gift to the generations to come. The tree planting that the Rambam imagined was a sign that Isaac now believed the land would belong to his seed as God had promised.

Isaac must have been consoled because now he had what his
father had, a woman of his own who would complete his torn
soul, making whole what had been ripped apart on Mount Moriah. Isaac was a quiet man. It's likely that he was not a man
who could see his animals slaughtered. He would have allowed
his servants and his slaves to do the work of death. He may
never have picked up a knife. Perhaps he was a shepherd whose
flock would come at his call. Perhaps he carried a hurt lamb on
his shoulders when his bondsmen said to kill it. He nursed it
himself and warmed it in his cloak. When it regained its
strength he thanked God.

Isaac was consoled because his wife was his mirror, his wife
was his female self, his wife was his mother returned, his wife
had changed the night from a time to rest into a time to embrace all the flowing energy of his body. She would not have
minded if he smelled of the field or the sweat had not been
washed from his skin. She would not have minded if he woke
with nightmares. She must have called him beloved, and he
must have believed he was.

Rashi said, "It is human nature that as long as a man's
mother is alive he is involved, entangled with her but when she
dies, he comforts himself in his wife."

If Rebekah asked him about Mount Moriah he would have
said nothing. It's likely that she would never know that Satan
had come to him and urged him to flee. She would never know
that, as one sage said, he had laid himself down on the firewood

and asked his father to bind his hands so he wouldn't struggle
and be cut, and in so doing make the sacrifice less than perfect,
less than it should be. (Animal sacrifices were rejected when
torn, cut, or bruised. Only the perfectly whole could be offered to the diety.)

By tradition, Isaac is considered to be gentle and unassum-
ing. His role in the story is not heroic in the usual meaning of
the word. At the important moment of passing on the inheritance of Abraham he is blind, and his second son is able to fool
him. But Isaac is holy, pure, dear to God, who tested his father's faith with Isaac's own life. The story of Isaac being
taken up to Paradise is a telling one. After his experience on
Mount Moriah he is not entirely of this world anymore. He was
part holy spirit. While he lived out his mortal days his special
purity would have been known and cherished by Rebekah. The
radiance of those who know God would have been understood
by her, and perhaps her love for him, entwined with his closeness to God, brought her nearer than most of us ever come to
the Creator, to the mysteries of heaven and earth.

Rebekah, like Sarah before her, was barren. Year in and year
out, month after month she waited for the signs to appear, the
fullness of breast, the end of her bleeding, the sweet faintness
in the early morning, but they did not. She prayed to God, but
He did not answer her. She walked out among the bondswomen and the slaves and saw that they conceived, child after
child. She must have held the babies of other women and
touched the soft space at the top of their heads, and she longed

for her own child. She must have longed and she must have hoped and then despaired.

Some say nineteen years passed and she was no longer young and firm and no longer did she raise her arms to the heavens and smile at all she saw around her. But perhaps it was only a matter of a few years. It was likely enough time to cause her to sit sadly inside her tent. Isaac must have known what she wanted and what she did not have. He too wanted sons. It had been promised to his father that his seed would continue, and he believed that it would, in time, just as it had with his mother, but when he told Rebekah this, she may have pulled away from him.

Rebekah prayed to God, begging Him to open her womb. He did not. Why? she asked him. What have I done to be punished so? There was no answer. The sages said that some scholars believed that Rebekah's brother Laban had cursed her when she left his household because he had wanted a richer bride price than had been paid, or because he was jealous of her good fortune, or because, as future tales would tell, he was a man who could let no one leave without gouging them, hounding them, hurting them. The curse was said to lie in the sarcastic way he blessed her. It was said that Laban's curse disguised as a blessing kept her barren.

There is no real evidence that shows Laban's blessing was said with sarcasm, but we are always trying to create causes for our misfortune, because it is painful, accepting the random cruelty of fate.

Genesis 25:21: "And Isaac pleaded with the Lord on behalf of his wife for she was barren, and the Lord granted his plea, and Rebekah his wife conceived."

Legend tells us that Rebekah asked Isaac, who never asked God for anything, who never spoke to God except in formal phrases of praise for His kindness to the world of His creation, to pray to the Lord on her behalf. He was reluctant. He told her to pray for herself. She said she had prayed and her prayers had not been answered. Was Isaac afraid that if he had a son God would demand him as a blood offering? A man can long for something and fear it at the same time.

She must have asked him again and again.

Then Isaac prayed to the Lord to give Rebekah a child. He may have whispered his prayer. He was not a man to feel entitled, to be sure of his rights, to call in a debt that the Lord might have incurred on Mount Moriah. He may have asked the Lord to do this thing in honor of his father Abraham so that the word of the Lord could be fulfilled and that a mighty nation could spring from his loins. Isaac may have kissed the stone on which he was kneeling. He may have put his forehead down on the damp earth. Maybe he did not expect that God would heed him. But he loved Rebekah and must have wanted her to be consoled by a child, as he had been consoled by her.

One of the sages said that Rebekah and Isaac knelt on the ground opposite each other and prayed to the Lord for a child, and it was this combined effort that reached into the heavens and was heard. Another sage said that Isaac prayed that the children he was destined to have would come from Rebekah's womb. Rebekah prayed that the children she was destined to have would only be Isaac's. Isaac's prayer was answered because he was a righteous man who was the son of a righteous man, whereas Rebekah's prayer was ignored because she was from a wicked family. Perhaps this is an example of a male protecting the assumed special male relationship with God, or perhaps it is just an expression of the importance of family lines in these stories. Good is assumed to be inherited, and evil too is passed on through the generations.

But God may have needed Isaac to make the plea in his own name. It was important that Isaac not serve as a hole over which the generations would leap but as a man who would take his place among the remembered, among the vital, among the fathers of the nation. He needed Isaac to believe not only in his own life but also in the future, the story that would go on without him. He needed Isaac to claim his part in the tale. If he held back, forever bound on the pile of firewood at Mount Moriah, then God could not make of him a nation, strong and willing, a nation that would be seared on its own firewood many times before the story would end.

It says in Genesis 25:21 only that "the Lord granted his plea and Rebekah his wife conceived."

Isaac's prayers were answered, and within a month Rebekah must have found a new lightness in her limbs, a hope that she kept secret, but a hope nevertheless, one that grew each day as she felt the tenderness in her breasts, the swirling in her head. Her eyes may have begun to shine as they had when she'd arrived from Paddan-aram.

The sages asked, "Why were the mothers so long barren?" They answered themselves. "Because the Holy One blessed be

He, longed to hear their prayer. He said to them 'My Dove, I will tell you why I have kept you childless. Because I was yearning to hear your prayer—as it is written, for your voice is sweet and your face is comely.' " Only a sage without a wife or a sister could have made that particular statement. It assumes that God plays with the human heart as if it were a toy on His shelf. God could not have been cruel enough to cause suffering only to hear the laments of his wounded creatures. He must have had a better reason.

Certainly conception is a common enough nonmiraculous event. Only by withholding pregnancy from the most central women in this story could it be made clear that God alone is the instrument of human survival, the grantor of our deepest wishes, the source of life itself. The long period of childlessness that afflicted Sarah and Rebekah and then Rachel is not a test of their patience and virtue, not a plot device to create suspense and difficulty, but a proof that God is ever the giver of life and man is ever the supplicant, and that the nation of people that God had selected to fulfill his plans would disappear in an instant were it not for the divine affection that has surrounded them through their days.

Genesis 25:22 says, "And the children clashed together within her and she said, 'Then why me?' And she went to inquire of the Lord, and the Lord said to her:

'Two nations—in your womb.
Two peoples from your loins shall issue

People over people shall prevail
The older, the younger's slave.'"

*M*any people believe that an angel watches over each pregnancy. This is an angel who guides women who might have lost their balance over the path so they do not fall. This is an angel who hums songs in the woman's ear so the baby inside will not become restless and exit before its time. The angel must have tried to sooth the twin boys in Rebekah's womb, but it was impossible, so terrible was the trouble between them.

A sage tells the story, a story that jumbles historical time, that Rebekah in her pain had gone to see Shem, the son of Noah, now the chief rabbi of a famous yeshiva. He had said, in echo or translation of God's speech to Rebekah, "Each of the twins will found a nation. The two will be unable to live together. The rise of one will mean the other's decline." Perhaps this story was there because it seemed wrong to some early reader that the Lord had actually spoken to Rebekah, considering that He was so sparing of His voice and she was a woman.

Rebekah must have been afraid for both her sons, and while she may have begun here to understand her special place in the history of her people, at the same time she would have been no more than an ordinary mother, waiting for her two babies to come forth, love for them growing each day.

Why was this struggle in Rebekah's womb necessary? Wasn't there space enough in God's creation for two nations to find land and water, harvest and trade? Was peace among the peoples a miracle beyond God's power?

Some say that Satan was helping Esau in the womb attempt

to strangle Jacob and that God sent an angel to protect Jacob and keep him alive. This was the struggle that caused Rebekah's pain.

Another sage said that each time Rebekah would pass a house of worship, Jacob would fight in the womb to emerge, and each time she passed a shrine to an idol Esau would thrust himself forward attempting to get out.

The pain did not stop, but now Rebekah may have understood its source. This was to be a special birth, two children, two nations, and she their mother. She may have thanked God for granting her this role, for speaking to her on the hilltop, for taking pity on her confusion, for giving her two sons, for sparing Isaac on Mount Moriah, because if He hadn't then there would be no further stories, all would have ended there. She would have been married to another man, a man without a star following his every step, an ordinary man who would give her ordinary children. There is no record of her telling Isaac what the Lord told her.

God spoke to Rebekah and revealed the future. It is her sons who will be envious of each other, who will threaten each other's very breath. It will be her efforts that will bring the story forward. Brother against brother they will forge the nation that will arise from their conflict.

The Lord had spoken to Abraham and indirectly to Sarah through a visiting angel, or perhaps it was his own voice, but he had no important message that was meant for Sarah alone. It was to Rebekah he revealed the destiny of her children, perhaps because he trusted her love as a mother to keep both of them alive, perhaps because he knew she would be strong enough to ensure that the seed of the Jewish nation would continue uncorrupted by idol worship, and her descendants would remain upright and God loving. Isaac, who had escaped death on Mount Moriah, was like a branch on a log that had been through a fire. The twig may have stayed green, but it was dried at the root, ash lay in the grooves of its bark. The task of assuring the proper succession was left to Rebekah.

Also it is the way with sons to murder and rob each other. It is the way of mothers to grieve for both, to watch with wet eyes, to hide in the rubble, to bind wounds, to pass the days in anxious ignorance of the fate of their children. It may have been for this reason that God spoke to Rebekah. She needed to hear His voice more than anyone on earth.

Cain against Abel, Ishmael against Isaac, nation against nation: this is not an unfamiliar world.

*G*enesis 25:24: "And when her time was come to give birth, look, there were twins in her womb. And the first one came out ruddy, like a hairy mantle all over and they called his name Esau. Then his brother came out, his hand grasping his heel, and they called his name Jacob."

It may have been like this: when the time came at last, after Rebekah's feet had swollen so large she could hardly walk, after her back ached, after she wept with exhaustion when she simply took the pots to the river to wash them, after she was kicked from within a million times, and after all the pain of the pushing and pulling, she did indeed break her water, call for the servant to help her, lie down on her bed, and call on the Lord to comfort her through the ordeal ahead, for this birth would not be easy.

She was brave, the way every woman is brave in childbirth. As God told Eve, they would come in pain, splitting apart the organs of life within, pain that came and went despite the midwife's herbal potion, despite changing positions, despite her cries. The two babies pushed against each other, delaying their passage through the birth canal. They turned and flailed; each was caught in the cord of the other and then released themselves. It may have begun at dawn and lasted until the following dawn.

Isaac must have walked outside her tent, and his breath was short. There was nothing he could do.

We do not know if Rebekah thought of the dangers to herself and her babies that the moments of birth had brought. But surely she knew that many women and many infants do not survive. Again and again women risked losing everything for the sake of the next generation, for the sake of a small infant seeking light and air down a dark passageway.

Some say that Esau was so rough that he tore Rebekah's womb so she could have no more children. The sages report that Rebekah was destined to give birth to twelve sons, who would in time become the twelve tribes of Israel. But because of Esau's roughness the tribes would have to wait for another generation. It is said that Jacob was conceived first and Esau second, because the second child would be born first if both were packed into a small space. The sages said that the Angel

Michael came down to earth and pushed Jacob through the birth canal. Another sage tells us that as they moved forward the boys struggled, each eager to be the first to draw a breath, the first to let out a cry, the first to see their mother's face. The sages say the fight between them was terrible, but when Jacob realized that the battle would kill his mother, he gave way in order to save her, as a good son would.

A legend tells us that Jacob was born circumcised, as were only twelve other saints in Jewish biblical history.

Afterward Rebekah must have felt what all new mothers feel, satisfaction, hope, a conviction that all was well, all was good and always would be. Isaac was sixty years old.

Perhaps Isaac thanked Rebekah for his sons, the ruddy one and the other, the pale one. The entire camp must have celebrated. They drank the wine that they had made from the grapes. They roasted lambs and they feasted as they shared Rebekah's and Isaac's joy. Rebekah forgot the pain of birth. Rebekah forgot the pain of the months before the birth. But she did not forget the Lord's words to her.

Despite the sages conjectures about the Angel Michael, we have no record of meteors charging through the heavens or moons slipping out of place. We have no record of huge winds or rains or unnatural doings. There is no certainty that any angels attended the birth, or that any powerful lords came to the bedside. The birth seems to have been like other births, marked by those in the small camp of the Israelites, longed for by the mother and father whose hands touched the babies' heads, who listened to the new drawing of breath and gave thanks and yet in the cry of these infants, in the sweet kisses of their mother, was promised the future of the nation, its moral purpose, its best stories to come.

*T*he babies suckled one at each breast and they grew. When they were little the differences between them were few. The sages say they were like the myrtle and the thornbush, which look alike in the early stages of their growth. After they have reached full size, the myrtle is known by its fragrance and the thornbush by its thorns.

Each brother loved his mother, and the mother loved them both, but it was clear that one was kind and the other was rough. The kind one needed her protection from the rough one. Yes he was the younger by a few seconds, but more importantly he was the one whose eyes shined when they walked together to see the morning dew on the bushes.

Rebekah must have understood that both boys were needed to tell the story that they were born to tell. She knew she must raise them both to manhood, that was what God expected of her.

The days were not so different one from another. The seasons changed, the camp moved north or south, looking for greener grasses. The seeds for the wheat were placed in the ground, and the seeds for the barley followed. The animals were sheared and slaughtered and the fires were lit for cooking, and the boys grew taller. Esau learned to shoot with arrows and Jacob learned to tend the ewes when they were delivering their young, and Rebekah must have told both of them to thank

God every morning for figs, dates, pomegranates, oranges that fell from the bushes all around. She taught them to thank God for the warmth of the sun and the sweetness of night, which embraced them while they slept.

Rebekah would have settled disputes between the servants. She would have made the slaves comfortable in their tents. Perhaps she healed the leg of one with an ointment made of bark and fat from a boar. She wove cloth for cloaks from sheeps' wool. She made the fire and she cleaned away the ashes. She would have wanted more children, but that was not possible.

It must have been that Esau was bigger, and he walked before the other. But Jacob stayed near his mother and called her name first. Esau chased the rabbits in the field and he threw stones at them. Jacob sat still and watched the small fish in the stream and left grain for the birds to eat.

Most likely Rebekah waited anxiously for Esau when he went deep into the forest and did not return for a fortnight, and she prayed over Jacob when he grew hot with fever and lay in his bed for many days. He learned quickly all she could teach him.

Most likely sometimes she ached for her own mother, wishing she could see her once more, but the boys grew strong and the herds increased.

Isaac must have come to her at night, and there was peace in the house.

The birthright and the larger portion of the inheritance belonged to the eldest son. It was the eldest who would be the head of the household when his time came and claim the cattle, the slaves, the camels, the gold. The older of the two boys was Esau and the right belonged to him. By only a second it is true, but that second mattered as much as a year or perhaps a lifetime.

*G*enesis 25:27 says, "And Esau was a man skilled in hunting, a man of the field, and Jacob was a simple man, a dweller in tents and Isaac loved Esau for the game that he brought him, but Rebekah loved Jacob." The word *simple* can be translated as "innocent." Actually as Robert Alter, the translator of the Five Books of Moses, says, Jacob was neither innocent nor simple. Had he been, we would have had no story, no nation.

Esau grew to love the hunt and he was swift and strong and could shoot his arrow with accuracy. As soon as he reached his full strength he was able to carry home to his father deer and boar, wild turkeys, ibexes, and the occasional panther or wolf whose skin he would carefully prepare for garments. His father was grateful for the bounty of the forest that his son harvested. Perhaps he would run his hands over the boy's head and draw him into his chest.

Jacob on the other hand, although also strong of build, with arms that could lift logs and pull up trees, preferred to tend the flock, to help the ewes give birth, to stay nearer the tent of his mother. Most likely Jacob's eyes had a faraway look. He woke in the morning and thanked God for the first pale light of dawn. A sage said he studied the stars and learned their patterns.

Several sages said that Isaac favored Esau because he saw in his hunter-son the man that he himself was not.

Jacob's will was turned to God.

The sages said that Jacob studied the law while Esau went into the forests and began to frequent Canaanite shrines. It was said by several of these same sages that before the age of twenty, Esau had committed murder, rape, robbery, and sodomy. Another sage said that God blinded Isaac so that he wouldn't see the silent reproaches of his neighbors who suffered from the acts of his son. But the sages had an interest in telling us of Esau's terrible deeds. They serve to justify Jacob's theft of the inheritance from his older brother and to enhance the virtue of the man who was destined to become one of the fathers of the Jewish nation.

There is a story by a sage writing centuries later that Esau subjected himself to a painful operation to hide his circumcision. This was a slander against Esau but one that revealed the fear of many in the nation, which was then in exile, that some would turn their back, betray their tradition, leave the fold, become idol worshippers. Esau became the example of the path not to take, the one to despise, the evil that was Cain and not Abel. This may not have been fair. Perhaps Esau was not as smart as his brother, or as loyal to his kind, but was he such a monster? Could Esau have been libeled?

Abraham died at the age of 175 years. His sons Isaac and Ishmael laid him to rest beside his wife Sarah in the cave of Machpelah. The legend is told that Abraham celebrated the feast of the first fruits with Jacob at Hebron, offering sacrifices at the altar he had built there. Rebekah had baked cakes of newly harvested corn, and Jacob took them to Abraham, who as he ate gave God thanks for his happy lot. He blessed Jacob and bequeathed him the house near Damascus. Jacob then embraced his grandfather and fell asleep in his arms. When he awoke his grandfather was no longer alive. Legend tells us that Abraham insisted on seeing the entire world before he would consent to die, and the cherubim drew him across the heavens in a chariot. A sage said that Abraham died five years earlier than he might have because God did not want him to see Esau's wicked deeds.

*R*ebekah preferred her other son, the one who must have asked questions, who would have made plans for the harvest long before the season arrived. She knew Jacob was devoted to the one true God, and she knew he would protect those who belonged to him from danger. She might still have loved Esau, and understood that he was, like the land itself, wild and eager, abundant in its richness, terrible in its fierceness. She might have loved Esau, but in the other one she saw the word of God, as well as the future of the people who obeyed that God.

Rebekah was the mother of two children, but she had also been God's choice for Isaac, God's choice for the nation that was to come, the nation that would follow the word of God most of the time, as best as human beings can. This meant that she had to do more on this earth than most. Merely loving her children would not suffice. She would have to choose between them; only one could be the hero of the story. It seems now as if the choice were simple. But this choice could not have been made without pain. But she never forgot the words of the Lord: "the elder the younger's slave."

Perhaps it would have been better if no one were anyone's slave. Perhaps it would have been better if the Lord had shared his blessings for both and if Isaac had divided his inheritance equally between his sons, but that was not the divine plan, nor was it the way of man in the land of Canaan in a time before this time. Perhaps human beings were too rough of soul, or still bruised from the exit from the Garden of Eden. Rebekah had to make a choice, but before she did, Jacob took matters into his own hands.

*E*sau had been out hunting many days, and he had been unsuccessful because the animals were birthing deep in caves and nothing had come across his path. He returned empty-handed. Jacob had been preparing a stew of red lentils.

Genesis 25:30: "And Esau said to Jacob, 'Let me gulp down some of this red stuff for I am famished.' . . . Jacob said, 'Sell now your birthright to me.' And Esau said, 'Look, I am at the point of death, so why do I need a birthright?' " He agreed to sell his birthright in return for a bowl of lentil beans. A sage pointed out that the word *gulping* in Hebrew is the word used for feeding animals. Therefore the sages concluded Esau was crude and primitive and like a beast.

Another sage suggests that Jacob, seeing that Esau had won his father's heart with food, tried to compete by preparing his own hearty vegetarian offering.

There is a legend that tells the story another way. Esau had just ambushed King Nimrod, the same Nimrod who had tried to kill Abraham and was still alive at age 215. The king had envied Esau his reputation as a hunter and had tried to kill him. After Nimrod was pierced by one of Esau's arrows Nimrod's men pursued Esau into the forest. They did not give up easily and chased him for many days. This is what reduced Esau to such a desperate state of weakness and hunger. It was said that the angels Michael and Gabriel witnessed the signing of the contract in which Esau agreed to forfeit his birthright for a bowl of lentil stew.

Genesis 25:33: "And Jacob said, 'Swear to me now,' and he swore to him and he sold his birthright to Jacob. Then Jacob gave Esau bread and lentil stew, and he ate and he drank and he rose and he went off, and Esau spurned the birthright." Legend says that when Esau had gone off Jacob laughed and said, "My brother despises his birthright."

Jacob must have told his mother about the sale of the birthright. Likely he did not tell his father. She did not tell her husband. Rebekah may not yet have decided what to do. She may have hoped that Isaac himself as he grew old would see that Jacob was the son who should inherit all and was the true heir to Abraham and the promises God had made to his descendants.

*T*here was a famine in the land. The sun had reappeared in the sky day after day. The clouds that passed released no rain. The streams dried to dust, the rivers shrank to streams. The fish in the waters died on the banks. The deer grew thin and their bones could be seen. The olives grew small as nuts on the trees, and the grain withered. In addition the men of the land laid waste to their neighbors' fields. They were ready to take from others what the land had denied them. The fields were trampled and the storage pits were robbed. Slaves were sent away to die, and the neighboring women were abused in the unrelenting heat of noon. It is said in the Zohar that famine comes only when mercy ceases to temper justice.

Isaac decided to break camp and move with his people and his herds like his father Abraham before him. This story has echoes in other stories. Everywhere there are events that recall other events, tales that are similar but slightly changed. It's as if the narrator's voice ricocheted back and forth among the hills. Isaac considered moving down to Egypt, where it was said the land was blessed with blue water and the grass was green.

Genesis 26:1: "And the Lord appeared unto him and said, 'Do not go down to Egypt. Stay in the land that I shall say to you. Sojourn in this land so that I may be with you and bless you and I will fulfill the oath that I swore Abraham your father, and I will multiply your seed like the stars in the heavens and I will give to your seed all these lands and all the nations of the earth shall be blessed through your seed because Abraham has listened to my voice.' "

Isaac did not go to Egypt but stopped at Gerar. Rebekah came into the city gates with him, and the men all observed her great beauty and they asked Isaac, Who is this woman? And he said, "She is my sister." Like his father, Abraham, in another place at another time, he feared that he would be killed because she was so lovely.

Rebekah heard him say this and most likely she was not surprised.

Rebekah surrounded herself with her servants and she veiled herself. She walked forward cautiously. The men around her were wolves with their tongues hanging out, eager to attack, to disgrace her, to defile her and perhaps to kill her, as if she were no more than a calf that had come to their hearth. She went to the tent that had been prepared for her not far from the home of King Benmelech, son of Abimelech, king of the Philistines. (Though Genesis refers to this King Benmelech as Abimelech, the sages assume that Benmelech was Abimelech's son.) Perhaps she had the servant bring her a sharp knife. She could not run fast enough to escape a pursuer. She could not bite or claw him to death, but she could use a knife. The knife was under her pillow.

But more important than the knife, she must have known she had the Lord on her side. She must have believed that He would not abandon her here in Gerar. She must have felt His presence, even though she did not hear His voice. She must have been wary and patient and prepared.

Time drew on. The men of the place did not grab Rebekah. They bided their time. Perhaps they thought about it, each of them privately, but they waited. Rashi points out that Isaac must have grown complacent with the passage of time, assuming he did not have to be so careful because Rebekah had not been raped.

Perhaps they walked together a little away from the tent.

She leaned against a sycamore tree. Then she ran from him and he chased her. There was laughter. He caught her in his arms. They kissed the way lovers do, the way husbands and wives do when they both want each other immediately. There may be all that in the word *playing*.

Out of his window the king saw them. Genesis 26:8: "That Abimelech king of the Philistines looked out the window and saw—there was Isaac playing with Rebekah his wife." He had been tricked. This was not the way a brother acted toward a sister. Immediately he summoned Isaac to come to him. The king said to Isaac, Genesis 26:9, " 'Why look she is your wife. How dare you say, "She is my sister." ' And Isaac said to him, 'For I thought, lest I die over her.' And Abimelech said, 'What is this you have done? One of the people might well have lain with your wife and you would have brought guilt upon us.' "

Adultery was a great sin. It was supposed that the entire moral order would be undone if a man and a woman had sex out of marriage. It was assumed that the Lord God or the many gods of the pagan world would take revenge on the community, ruin the crops, bring disease, open the gates to the enemy, if such a sin were committed. So this Abimelech-Benmelech issued a command to all his people that if anyone harmed Isaac or his wife, Rebekah, they would be doomed to die.

This story was written down centuries later as the justification for the use of deception when Israelites are in danger abroad. Sometimes deceit is necessary for survival. It is one of the few weapons in the arsenal of the powerless. This tale explains that God understands that men have to lie and women have to scheme because survival is a more important value than truth. All across the ancient world trickery was practiced and understood as necessary in times of trial. The Greeks tricked the Trojans with their horse. Odysseus tricked the Cyclops. Prometheus stole fire. The snake tricked Eve. Abraham lied to Sarah when he took Isaac to the mountain. Rebekah did not tell Isaac of the prophesy about her sons. There was no value then placed on honesty between man and wife, man and man. In a world where one had all the rights and the other only her sharp eye and her sleight of hand, it was no wonder that honesty was of no more use than the bones of the fish cooked last night in the fire.

The Lord blessed Isaac and he prospered.

A sage said about Isaac's wealth, "Rather the dung of Isaac's mules than all Benmelech's gold and silver." Isaac had the virtue of Abraham planted in his soul. Benmelech only had wealth. But then Isaac too acquired great wealth. His animals increased, his possessions became numerous, and he had many slaves. And now a problem that has plagued the nation through the following millennia appears. The Philistines envy Isaac because of his wealth and good fortune. Genesis 26:16 says, "Abimelech said to Isaac, 'Go away from us, for you have grown too powerful for us.'"

Isaac then went into the wadi of Gerar and set up his tents there, and he dug open the wells that had been opened by his father Abraham, which the Philistines had blocked up with shovelfuls of dirt and debris after Abraham's death, fearing no retribution, fearing only the return of Abraham's family. Now there was enough water for all the animals because

Isaac dug up the wells that Abraham, his father, had first found.

And then came a time when the Philistines grew even more envious of Isaac's good fortune. After all he was a stranger among them. He worshiped a God whom he claimed was the only God. His prosperity mocked their many gods, whom they both feared and loved, and to whom they sacrificed their best lambs and brought the first fruits of their harvest. Here was Isaac, his flock increasing, water on his land, his family strong and healthy. Of course they did not welcome him or wish him to stay in their midst. Here starts the familiar whispers: "Isaac owns everything. Isaac is selfish. He is corrupt. He should leave our place and go somewhere else." Rebekah must have heard the whispers.

Soon the shepherds of Gerar quarreled with Isaac's shepherds, saying in Genesis 26:20, "The water is ours."

The famine in the land of Canaan was over. Isaac and Rebekah packed their tents. They traveled a long distance home. God spoke to Isaac the very night that they arrived, weary from the long journey. He said to Isaac, "I am the God of Abraham your father. Fear not for I will bless you and I will multiply your seed for the sake of Abraham my servant." Isaac built an altar there. Perhaps Rebekah believed that Isaac was beloved of the Lord because of the sweetness of his heart.

Several weeks later Benmelech came to him from Gerar with his councillor and a hundred armed men. Isaac's servants and his slaves took up their swords. Some of their men were away from the tents, looking for water. Most likely Rebekah kept her boys hidden in a tent. Perhaps holes were dug in the grass, and bracelets and trinkets, gold bars and favorite pots, were buried and covered with grass and weeds and rocks.

Isaac sat down with Benmelech and his men and, in Genesis 26:22, "said to them, 'Why have you come to me when you have been hostile toward me and have sent me away from you?' and they said, 'We have clearly seen that the Lord is with you and we thought—let there be an oath between our two sides, and let us seal a pact with you.' " Word must have spread through the camp that the hostile visitors had come seeking a treaty. Then perhaps the women emerged and the children rushed out to see the strangers, and food was prepared and brought to the men. Isaac must have sent a message to Rebekah asking her to come to his side.

As the feast was ending long after darkness had come, some of Isaac's men who had been away from camp arrived and joined the men, still drinking and eating, plates and bones, cups and vessels scattered around the fires. Isaac's men had found water. Isaac called the well Sheba and the place became known as Beer Sheba.

Without the wells the flocks could not survive the long dry months. Without the wells the wives and children could not drink and wash and cast off the sickness of summer and the sickness of winter. Without water the camels would sink to their knees and die. Without water the land was of no use. God had promised Isaac the land and promised him that his seed would prosper, so while Isaac made a treaty with Benmelech, the Lord must have led the servants to water, cool rushing water that could be gathered in a pool, replenished each day from the miraculous spring beneath the ground. Water, like fire, runs through the history of the people. Moses is saved by being floated in a basket along the Nile. The slaves of Pharaoh are blocked by the sea, but miraculously it parts for them, so they can escape. Pharaoh's army is drowned in the sea.

Perhaps that night Rebekah anointed herself with oils.

Legend tell us that after Benmelech returned to Gerar, bandits sacked his royal treasure-house, taking away silver and gold, goblets and necklaces, ruby rings and wealth gathered over the years. Benmelech woke the next morning to find sores on his skin. He called the royal doctor, who whispered in his ear the terrible news that the king had become a leper. Then the wells dried up. The people of Gerar were hungry. The crops failed one after another. When Isaac departed from Gerar the good fortune of the Philistines fled, or so this legend says. In fact, however, when God's people were driven in the following centuries from one place or another it was rare that retribution followed.

*E*sau married. He was forty years old, the sages say, old enough to marry. The sages considered that his marriage was done at the right time of his life, but they didn't like him anyway. One said that Esau was like a swine who stretches out its feet when it lies down, to show that it is cloven-footed like the clean animals, though it is nonetheless one of the unclean because it doesn't chew its cud, a matter of Kosher law. But Esau's choice of brides caused Rebekah and Isaac grief. He married two women, which was not against custom. He chose Judith,

the daughter of Beeri the Hittite, and Basemath, the daughter of
Elon the Hittite. These young women were raised to worship
the local gods, the fertility goddess, the war god, the god of
crops. They were accustomed to the ways of pagans and they
did not intend to change. Esau was not a man to mind. He
prayed little himself. He preferred to rely on his strong arm and
his strong back and his way with animals in the woods. He must
have been interested in the smell and the look and the willingness of his wives, not their belief in one kind of god or another.

The desire of a man to marry a woman from another culture is as old as the sands of Sinai. The woman may be available, perhaps exotic, willing, and the beauty of a stranger
always appears greater than the beauty of the familar. But the
people will not be the same when the tribal lines are crossed,
when the children belong to both groups, when the mother can
whisper into the child's ear, do this or that—for this or that
god who will reward you for your effort. To keep in mind the
one true God—the one unifying God who has a moral vision
of the universe, who commands and demands moral behavior
from his folk—was difficult. The sternness of it, the simplicity
of it, could easily be overcome by the joy in wild festivals, the
fascination of dark sacrifices, the wild dreams and fabulous stories. The love of the one God could easily be erased by a warm
breast and the eager arms of a follower of a more congenial religious order, or it could be erased, out of indifference, or it
could be abandoned because it was too much trouble.

Rebekah and Isaac must have known that their numbers
were few. They lived in the land that the Lord had promised
them, but others with very different views lived there too,

bought their blankets, traded pots and trinkets with them, weighed their grain in silver ingots, and piled up gold in boxes. They knew that others who did not follow their God could easily swallow up their people, causing the tale begun by Abraham to end before it had begun. For reasons that Rebekah might have hardly understood, that Isaac may have never formed into words, they believed such a loss would be tragic, would betray all they found meaningful, all that they had worked for, as they gathered wealth, raised their children, worked with their hands day by day, and offered prayers in the hopes they held for the future of their kind.

They believed that such a severance would signal a darkening of the sky, a weakening of the human endeavor, a cowardice in the face of hard times. How important to them it must have been that the line of Abraham continue and with it the worship of the Lord as they understood Him—one mighty force in a universe, the Creator of all things. He had spoken to them, granted their prayers, protected them from bandits and jealous neighbors. So much had been endured for His sake.

When Esau married Basemath and Judith, Rebekah may have laid down on her bed and turned her head away from Isaac. She may have been silent for days. She was surely bitter. The idiolatry of her daughters-in-law disturbed her greatly. Genesis 26:35 says, "And they were a provocation to Isaac and to Rebekah."

*I*saac had grown old and his eyes were dim. He must hardly have left the tent now, and only leaning on the arm of his wife, a servant at his other side. He may still have liked to go down to the spring and feel the fresh water coming from deep within the ground. But he could no longer see.

The sages said that when Isaac was bound on the altar, as Abraham lifted up his knife, the angels hovered above him, weeping, and their tears fell into Isaac's eyes, weakening them so that in old age he went blind.

Rebekah and Jacob must have together taken on the responsibilities of the family. Rebekah may have walked with her son Jacob each morning to the place where the camels rested. Perhaps she gave directions to the men who tended them. She went to the fields with the women and helped with the harvest of grain when it was ready. She may have gone to the well to bring water to the tent.

But she must have known that Isaac was weak and his breath was short and his time would soon end. This was her mate, the one God had chosen for her, and she must have been accustomed to the warmth of his body, accustomed to the film that covered his eyes. She must have been accustomed to his shadow, which she could see on the path.

Perhaps it was like this: Rebekah was outside the tent, pulling at the wool from a white sheep, dipping it in water and wringing it dry, when she heard Isaac calling out to Esau, who had come to bring his father the horns of a rhinoceros that could be sold in town for ingots of gold.

Genesis 27:2: "And it happened when Isaac was old, that his eyes grew too bleary to see, and he called to Esau his elder son and said to him, 'My son!' and he said, 'here I am.' And he said 'Look I am grown old; I know not how soon I shall die. So now, take up, pray, your gear, your quiver and bow and go out to the field and hunt me some game, and make me a dish of the kind that I love and bring it to me that I may eat, so that I may solemnly bless you before I die.' " Rebekah heard these words. She must have known this would happen one day.

Isaac was 123 years old. She did not intend to let him bless Esau with the blessing that would grant him all the inheritance, not just the worldly goods but also the promises from God that had been made to his grandfather and his father.

Over the years the sages have found it necessary to tell stories about Esau, how cruel he was, how he worshiped idols, how he lived like a brute among brutes. All this was written to build a wall around Jacob that the virtue of no other tribe could scale. It was written to make reasonable and sympathetic Rebekah's favoring of one child over the other. But Rebekah did not favor Jacob over Esau because Esau was evil or carried evil seeds within him. She favored Jacob because the Lord had told her the younger shall vanquish the elder. Rebekah favored Jacob because the nation was still forming and it needed one leader, one story, one hero, to carry forward the tale.

Rebekah favored Jacob and knew that her choice was the better choice. She was not ashamed of usurping Isaac's role. She was not ashamed of giving to one child at the expense of another, that was natural, it happened all the time, one way or the other. If the eldest took at the expense of the younger, was that more just, more pleasing to God? She thought not. Rebekah knew that the strongest in a litter would push the other away from the teat, and if God had minded this He would have created the litter equal or He would have provided ample nourishment for all. Rebekah knew that the loving hand of a mother sometimes gave a bigger portion to one child than to another. She knew that Jacob was the child that God wanted for His story, not the other one. It was her destiny to provide a means for Jacob to steal the blessing that granted the inheritance. She did.

What if she hadn't? God would have left His chosen people and perhaps picked another. God gave Rebekah the intelligence to think up the plot, the will to see her way to carry out the deception, the conviction to do what she thought was right. God knew that Rebekah there at the beginning of history made the right choice.

There are heros who saved the people by waging successful wars, like David and Samuel. There are heros, like the Maccabees, who won wars. There are heros who were martyred by torture, by fire, for the sanctification of the name, like Rabbi Ben Elizer, like the fighters in the resistance in the Warsaw Ghetto, but Rebekah was greater than them all because right there at the beginning she took the tapestry of Jewish history and saved it from unraveling. She had to act quickly and with conviction. She had no advisors and no friends and no angels speaking in her ear. She could not afford doubt. She had to act immediately, and she did.

In Genesis 27:9 Rebekah said to Jacob, " 'Go to the flock, and fetch me from there two choice kids that I may make them into a dish for your father of the kind he loves. And you shall bring it to your father and he shall eat, so that he may bless you before he dies." Jacob answered her. "Look, Esau my brother is a hairy man and I am a smooth skinned man. What if my father feels me and I seem a cheat to him and bring on myself a curse and not a blessing?" And his mother said, "Upon me your curse, my son. Just listen to my voice and go, fetch them for me."

Some people think that a curse can be deflected from its object if someone else accepts it in place of the cursed one. Who better than a mother to accept a curse intended for a child? How many mothers have prayed to the Lord to let them take their child's sickness, to take it off him and give it to them? How very natural it is for a mother to want a child's pain to be removed so much that she would plead for that pain to be given to her own body. Rebekah makes this promise sincerely enough, but at the same time she also knows it will convince her son to do her bidding.

She too is a great manipulator, which is a necessary gift if you are not the one with the power, not the one who gives orders but the one who receives them. What else could she do? Was there a more honest and direct way for a woman to turn a blessing from one son to another?

Jacob returned with the animals. Genesis 27:15 says, "And Rebekah took the garments of Esau her elder son, the finery that was with her in the house and put them on Jacob her younger son, and the skins of the kids she put on his hands and on the smooth part of his neck." Rebekah knew that animals often fell for this trick. If a ewe died and left nursing kids behind often the shepherds would put some fleece from another ewe's kids on the orphans so that the mother might be fooled into thinking these were her own and allow them to suckle also.

Genesis 27:17: "And she placed the dish and the bread she had made, in the hand of Jacob her son." A sage said that Rebekah accompanied Jacob as far as the door and then said to him, "This far I owed thee my aid, from here on outward the creator will assist thee!"

The sages (ignoring historical time) say that Jacob obeyed his mother because he honored her as the Fifth Commandment told him to, but he hated the deception, tears streaming from his eyes, and he inwardly prayed to God to remove this shame. But Rebekah knew that Jacob must face the ordeal and said: according to legend, "Courage my son! When Adam sinned was not Earth his mother, cursed? If needs be I shall tell your father that I have acted in my knowledge of Esau's evil ways."

The sages wondered how it was that Esau had left his clothes at his mother's house when he was married and had two wives. They explained that his wives were lazy as well as idolatrous and would not keep his clothes clean so he brought them to his mother. Some sages said that Esau's garments in which Rebekah clothed Jacob were those made by God for Adam and Eve, and now because Esau had sold his birthright these garments rightfully belonged to Jacob. Some sages say that Jacob obeyed his mother because he knew that he must but that he hated the deception and the theft that was about to occur, and that tears came to his eyes, and two angels had to support him as his legs grew weak as he entered the presence of his father.

Some of the Scholars who have poured over the texts have decided that Jacob had sinned in stealing the blessing that belonged to Esau, but in order to protect one of the founding fathers they deflected his sin onto his mother, saying that she forced him, she pulled him away from virtue, that a woman, once again, a woman like Eve, was the temptress that led the man away from God, toward the ways of Satan. Rebekah had after all agreed to take the curse that might fall on Jacob on her own soul. There were scholars who said that Jacob was bound to obey his mother's instructions, but he hated the part she forced on him and took great pains not to add any lies when he spoke to his father.

The Esau-Jacob story might have been cut altogether from the text that came down to us. When Jacob refuses to feed Esau, who is starving, he sins, and when Jacob deceives his father and steals the blessing from his brother he is hardly righteous. The editors of the story must have been disturbed. But the sages decided to use Jacob as an example of how to survive in a hostile world. The prophet Hosea had threatened the House of Israel with punishment for Jacob's evil deeds, and the second Isaiah later declares that Jacob's sin is at last punished by the Babylonian exile, when all the people marched by foot out of Jerusalem into Babylonia, leaving their beloved city behind and losing their land.

There is a similar story of a stolen blessing in non-Israelite Canaanite folklore that made its way into Greek myth. It was considered at that time that to be a man of many wiles, like the cruel and treacherous Odysseus, was noble and praiseworthy. But later, lies and stealing were strictly forbidden by Leviticus.

But this story is one in which real human behavior, not saintly behavior, is crucial. Without Rebekah the nation would not have been born, the will of God hidden forever. Without some stain on the human spirit there would be no story at all, no reason to read on, no reality to touch our hearts, no past to remember.

Why, the sages wondered, was Esau so delayed on his hunt that Rebekah had time to prepare her dish and Jacob time to go to the bedside of his father? A legend says that God sent an angel to go along with Esau on his hunt, and as each animal was killed and bound, the angel came and revived it and released it from its bonds. When Esau went back to pick up the animal it had disappeared. When Esau shot a bird and cut its wings, the angel repaired its wings so that it could fly away. He had to go farther and farther into the forest and still he had no animal in hand to bring back to his father.

Why was the second son favored over the firstborn? At first this seems strange in a culture where the birth order determined inheritance and where it was so firmly established that the first received all. In the end Isaac, who was the second son, received the inheritance. Jacob, who was the second son, stole the inheritance, and Rachel, who was the second daughter, received the love that perhaps belonged to her elder sister. Why do these stories consistently raise the younger over the older? Perhaps there was an identification of the tribe of Israel with the second son. After all they were the newcomers in the land. Perhaps there was an identification of monotheism, the love of one God instead of many, with the second son, since the religion of

Abraham had entered the land many generations after the worship of idols.

And then it may be that turning upside down the assumed order of succession reinforced the importance of personal merit. In a way, these stories may have contained a small burst of democratic hope pushing its way through the autocratic soil of the land. If Isaac and Jacob were more deserving than Ishmael and Esau then the prize should be theirs. Perhaps the rise of the second son is a sign that the sacred story is also about individual human moral quality, promising a world in which the stark lines of power could be altered and hope given to all that their time may come.

This is not to say that Genesis presents us with a democratic vision of society, only that humankind has long had a vision of a world that was not ruled by power alone and in which surprising events could occur, rewarding those who at birth had not been granted a high place.

Rebekah stood outside the tent flap while her son Jacob went in to his father. She listened. Genesis 27:18 says, "And he came to his father and said, 'Father!' and he said, 'Here I am. Who are you, my son?' And Jacob said to his father, 'I am Esau your firstborn. I have done as you have spoken to me. Rise, pray, sit up, and eat of my game so that you may solemnly bless me.' And Isaac said to his son, 'How is it that you found it so soon, my son?' And he said, 'Because the Lord your God gave me good luck.'" Isaac asked Jacob to come closer and he felt his hands covered in the skin of the kid and he was puzzled. Genesis 27:22–23: "And he said, 'the voice is the voice of Jacob and the hands are Esau's hands.' But he did not recognize him for his hands were, like Esau's hands, hairy, and he blessed him." Rebekah must have heard Isaac say, Genesis 27:25, "Are you my son Esau?" And she must have heard Jacob answer, "I am."

She must have been afraid. Was this what God had intended or was her plan a violation of His will? For a moment perhaps she expected punishment, instant punishment, but the sky was still, no angry voice roared, no darkening of the light. Perhaps she heard Isaac's shallow breathing. She heard the spoon against the edge of the bowl as her husband ate the dish she had prepared. Her eyes must have looked to the horizon. Would Esau come just at this moment and claim the blessing for himself?

Jacob picked up a goblet and poured wine for his father. The sages say that the wine that accompanied the dish that Rebekah had cooked had been brought to Jacob by the Angel Michael, who had been sent by the Lord to make sure all went well. Isaac took the wine to his father's side. Rebekah heard Isaac put down the wine. She heard Isaac request that Jacob come near him. Isaac was embracing Jacob. He would smell his clothes. Rebekah had known that Issaac would smell Jacob, and that is why she gave him Esau's garments to wear, despite the fact that Isaac could not see the clothes. The smell of game and sweat and grass stains soaked the robe that had belonged to Esau but was now worn by Jacob. Rebekah must have been afraid that now Isaac would discover the deception. But Isaac said, Genesis 27:27, "See, the smell of my son is like the smell of the field that the Lord has blessed." A sage said that the fragrances that came from Jacob that day came from the flowers in the Garden of Eden.

And then Rebekah listened as Jacob received his father's blessing, the one reserved for the firstborn. Genesis 27:28:

> *"May God grant you*
> *From the dew of the heavens and the fat of the earth*
> *May peoples serve you,*
> *And nations bow down before you.*
> *Be overlord to your brothers,*
> *May your mother's sons bow before you.*
> *Those who curse you be cursed,*
> *And those who bless you, blessed."*

Silently outside the tent Rebekah added her own blessing, or so the legend tells us. Rebekah said, "For He shall give His angels charge over you, to keep you in all your ways. They shall bear you up in their hands, lest you dash your feet against a stone. You shall walk upon the lion and the adder; the young lion and the serpent you shall trample under your feet."

It all happened quickly. Just a few hours had passed from Isaac's request to Esau, to Isaac's blessing of the son that he thought was Esau but was Jacob instead. The blessing had been given and could never be taken away.

Perhaps it was only then that Rebekah walked away. Only then did she straighten her spine and hold her head up again. She had given to Jacob the birthright that belonged to Esau. It was her plan. It was her sin. She must have understood that if in the future she was despised for this act she would have to bear it. If she had violated the natural order of elder over younger then she would have to be condemned. She must also have believed that she had done what God wished, what the oracle had said would be done, what needed to be done.

Perhaps, however, there was still some shame in her face? Perhaps she loved the son she had betrayed? Was this because a mother should never betray either child?

It happened of course all the time, the handsomer one received the larger portion of the sweets, the one that reminded the mother of a parent she loved received the hugs that should have been given to the other, and most all daughters received less than their brothers. If two brothers were drowning in the river and the mother could only save one, she saved her favorite and claimed it was the current that brought her to this one instead of that. The sages knew that this deed of Rebekah's, which was morally tainted, was the one that steered the people toward God.

Rabbi Gershom, son of Rabbi Akiva, said that, "It is both reasonable to assume and legal to believe that Esau hates Jacob. At the end of time Esau will wear a prayer shawl and take his place among the learned men and it will be God himself who throws him out."

A sage said that the exile of the Jews from Jerusalem when the Assyrians broke through the walls was a result of Rebekah's sin in betraying her son. Others said that the fall of the Temple in the time of the Romans was the Holy One's punishment on Rebekah for tricking Isaac. Some said that she was a woman who took into her own hands matters that were better left in God's. A great Hassidic master said that when Esau discovered that he had been cheated by Jacob and lost his blessing he shed two tears. It is because of these tears that the Jewish people were destined to shed so many more throughout the exile.

*E*sau had been hunting for game for over four hours and he found nothing. Then suddenly a deer appeared and he killed it and roasted it over the fire and prepared a dish for his father to eat. When Esau arrived bearing his offering to his father on a silver platter and asked his father for his blessing, his father realized what had happened. Genesis 27:33 says, "And Isaac was seized with a very great trembling." Esau must have wept bitter tears because Isaac could not take back his blessing and return it to his eldest son.

Rabbi Yohanon said that Essau committed five sins. He raped a girl who was already engaged to another man. He killed a man. He denied God's existence. He ridiculed the resurrection of the dead, and he gave up his birthright as firstborn. Perhaps this was so. Or perhaps the rabbi wanted to believe it was so in order to justify Rebekah and Jacob, who created the nation through an act of theft.

Isaac must have been afraid of the Lord God who had once ordered his death and would soon have it anyway. He did not expect a ram or an angel or his father's voice to save him this time. What was over was over, and he did not have the energy to fight his determined wife. His son Esau turned to him and

wept, and said, in Genesis 27:38, "Do you have but one blessing, my father? Bless me, too, father." He blessed him but not
with the blessing of the firstborn because that had already been
given. There was no comfort for Esau and no comfort for his
father either.

Rebekah's love of God was equal to Abraham's. One was
willing to sacrifice Isaac at the Lord's command, and the other
behind Isaac's back changed the order of things so they would
never again be the same. Isaac may have been loved by God
but he was not granted respect. He became a pawn in the story.
He was moved about the board by the hands of his wife and his
youngest son . . . others' hands. Rebekah, a woman, fooled
him and in doing so followed the will of God. Let no one say
that women had no role in the story.

The sages tell a story: when Esau entered his tent expecting
to receive his father's blessing, Isaac rose from his bed and saw
hell's fires burning at Esau's feet. He saw the flames licking at
Esau's legs, and he was afraid that he himself would be burned
in a terrible conflagration. But this vision of damnation is a
much later embroidery. Esau did not have to be evil for Jacob
to be the favorite in Rebekah's eyes. But it was far better for future generations to believe that Esau was Satan's child than
that Rebekah had favored Jacob without just cause.

There is a legend that says that Isaac grew angry when he
discovered the trick that had been played on him. He would
have cursed Jacob, but God warned him: "Did you not say 'let
your curser be cursed! Let your blesser be blessed.' Then Isaac
told Esau: 'While Jacob is worthy to be served, serve him you

must! But when he ceases to obey God's law, rebel and make him your servant.' "

When Rebekah entered the tent Isaac may have curled his hands into fists, but these were old man's fists. He may not have turned toward her voice. She would not have been surprised, but she would have known that he never stayed angry with her. He would want her to accompany him as far as possible into the grave.

*E*sau went off to the tents of his wives. He went home to his slaves and his servants. He must have howled into the heavens.

Esau's howl was a reproach to his mother. She must have heard his thoughts. His mother had placed his brother above him. A man cannot easily recover from this judgment. Rebekah may have wanted to console him, but she must have known that she should not go near him, not until his anger had cooled, not until Jacob was gone from their midst. And maybe not even then.

*R*ebekah had another plan. This one she may have held in her head a long time, before Isaac had lost his sight, long before it became clear that Esau was a man of ready emotions that swept over the land like thunder in a summer storm and Jacob was a man in his mother's image.

Perhaps she went to Jacob, who was pacing back and forth outside his tent, his sword in his hand, ready for Esau to attack, ready for all of Esau's servants to attack. He had packed his few garments, a ring of gold that his mother had given him, his small ax, his knives, the gold that was his, and he was trying to decide where to flee or whether to flee. Perhaps he should fight here and now. Esau was stronger, but Jacob was quicker. On the other hand perhaps he should go to the caves by Hebron, or the forests in the north, or to Ur, the land his grandfather had come from. This thing he had done, was it good? He could not have been certain. Guilt must have filled his heart with dread. Had he displeased his father and gained his blessing but lost his affection? Was God with him or did God now despise him?

His mother appeared before him and told him he must flee to her brother's house in Paddan-aram. Rebekah said to him, in Genesis 27:45, "Listen to my voice and rise, flee to my brother Laban in Haran, and you may stay with him a while until your brother's wrath subsides—and I shall send and fetch you from there. Why should I be bereft of both of you on one day?"

An Italian Scholar said Rebekah meant "I will be bereaved of both of you in one day because I will lose one and detest the other."

Jacob must have known that his mother was right. He needed to leave and as soon as possible. But he could not go without his father's blessing.

Isaac must have heard Rebekah's footsteps as she neared his bedside. She knew how to bring him to bless the journey Jacob must take. She said to Issac, Genesis 27:46, "I loathe my life because of the Hittite women! If Jacob takes a wife from the Hittite women like these, from the native girls, what good to me is life."

Here Rebekah brings Isaac to accept Jacob's departure and to bless him on his way. She claims that her grief is great over Esau's idolatrous wives and that she wants Jacob to marry from among her own people. Isaac can accept that. He too must want the family roots to stay strong. He too must dislike the women his son has married. With this cunning speech Rebekah provides Jacob with the blessing he needs in order to leave home, and at the same time, Robert Alter points out, she discredits Esau again, reminding Isaac that the son who did not receive his birthright was less worthy than the one who did.

A sage said that when Rebekah complained to Isaac about Esau's wives she did not mention them by name but blew her nose in a bitter rage and flung the snot from her fingers onto the ground. This undignified act does not seem to belong to the brave and determined spirit that belongs to Rebekah, our beautiful and clever Rebekah, a woman worthy of hearing God's voice, bearing God's chosen people. But what the sage's comment did report accurately was the bitterness of mothers whose daughters-in-law displeased them, came from another place, and worshiped other gods. The snot on the ground lies there still.

Isaac had not been a great prophet like his father. He had not been a great hunter like his son Esau. He had done little with his days but guard the wealth that Abraham had earned. He was blind, and he must now have needed the care of women, women who would help bathe him, bring him clothes, and put meat on the fire, chase away scorpions from the floor, and clap their hands at the bats that flew above whose wings he could hear but whose exact place he never knew.

Isaac must have known that there was one great thing in his life, one matter that made him a worthy man. It was not his miraculous birth and it was not his father, who had fulfilled God's promise, it was the life he had woven day after day with Rebekah, waking in happiness that she was by his side, lying down at night, certain that the Lord approved the work of his hands and the work of his heart. He agreed to Rebekah's plea to bless Jacob. He summoned Jacob and blessed him and commanded him, "You shall not take a wife from the daughters of Canaan. Rise go to Paddan-aram to the house of Bethuel your mother's father and take you from there a wife from the daughters of Laban, your mother's brother." Laban's wife, Adina, has given birth to two girls.

It must have been hard for Jacob to leave his parents' home. But it must also have been good to be setting out, to be at the beginning of one's own story. Surely it was with a strong step, with an eager eye, with his bow and arrow and his knives, with his camels and his goats and his cattle, with gold shekels, with grain in his sack, that he left the camp.

Rebekah may have stood on a hill and watched him disappear into the distant meadow. The grass was high and came up to his waist. Was the thing that she had done good in God's eyes or not? She hoped for a sign, a rainbow suddenly appearing, but there were no signs. She would have to comfort herself, be certain herself, silence her inner doubts with mockery, tend to Isaac in his last days.

She had at that time no more wisdom than the rest of us, no further access to God's voice, because He was finished with her. She had played her part in the story. She had only that resolve that was always with her. She would do, she would be, she would endure whatever came.

There is no record of her bitterness; no words of self-pity have lasted through the ages. She was a woman who begged for nothing for herself. But the sages in later years were concerned because Jacob must be a righteous man as the legitimate heir to God's promised land, and they placed the major part of the blame for his wrongdoing on the shoulders of his mother. She had in fact taken the curse on her own head.

As for Isaac, he died within weeks. One morning he simply did not wake. His old heart had stopped. His cloudy eyes remained closed. His hands reached for nothing. He was at peace. He was buried in the cave at Machpelah in a tomb not far from his father and mother's. Rebekah may have wept all the way there and needed to be supported by her handmaidens on the way back. She was far less strong without Isaac, she was half of herself, she was a map sketched in the dirt, rubbed out by the feet of the mapmaker when he was done.

Nevertheless as the years passed and Jacob did not return and she had little word of him, she likely grew more and more certain that all was well with him in a distant place. She would have watched Esau's children who laughed outside the tent as they played their games. She was not without comfort after all.

*T*he years went on. Rebekah herself became frail. Her heart skipped about in her chest. Her black hair turned gray. Her hands must have trembled when she removed a pan from the fire. Perhaps one night she lay on her bed and a great restlessness came upon her. She rose and walked out under the stars. She looked at the great dome of the heavens above her and she felt the ground under her feet. She felt very warm although the night was cold. Beads of sweat ran down her neck.

I have done all I had to do, she said to herself. I have finished with my life. And it was true. She turned back toward her tent. A pain seized her and she dropped to the ground and her heart cracked.

There is no mention in Genesis of her death. Some sages said that she had no funeral because of the shame that Esau had brought on the family. A funeral procession would bring out mockers, and people would throw things at her casket. Others say she had no funeral because there was no one of virtue to bury her. Jacob may not have heard of her death until many months afterward when a traveler came to Paddan-aram. Some say she had no funeral because her son Esau despised her and would allow no funeral for the mother who had betrayed him.

Some say the angels grieved for her, making wreaths of flowers that they flung across the land of Canaan. But maybe her handmaidens simply bore her to the cave at Machpelah, in the dark of night, when no one noticed, on the back of a donkey followed by a few of the men of her fields, the shepherds that cared for her flock and the keepers of her land. They climbed the hill to the field that had once belonged to Ephron the Hittite and now belonged to the descendants of Abraham and carried her in a wooden box, down into the cave at Machpelah, down its dark throat, through its first grotto into the place where Isaac lay across from his father and mother. There they put her with no words and no deep wailing. They may have left candles burning in the dark as a sign of respect. They must have left quickly. Although the smell in the air may have been sweet, it was not a place for breathing mortals.

There is a story that Rebekah was brought back from the dead and given to Job as his second wife, and she gave him many children and lived in undisturbed happiness.

Her life was what it was. She had died without seeing her son Jacob again, without knowing that he wrestled with an angel on a ladder, that he fathered twelve sons, that her people would be enslaved in Egypt and then return and then be defeated and then exiled more than once.

Each of us leaves the story before the end, the narrative goes on without us. There is nothing unusual about that.

Rachel
and Leah

WHAT IF THERE had been no story? No Abraham and Sarah, no Isaac and Rebekah, and no Esau and Jacob, and no Rachel and Leah. What if no one had remembered? What if no one had cared enough to write it down? What if there had been no God of Adam and Eve, Cain and Abel, and the ten generations from Noah to Abraham had never existed? What if there had been no creation and there was only chaos and the void? What if God himself was only a hole in the darkness?

Rachel and Leah, Leah and Rachel, sisters whose names are forever linked, who shared a husband, carried forward the history of the people. Perhaps theirs is the most sorrowful, complicated, crucial story of them all.

Legend tells us that Esau had sent his oldest son, Eliphaz, to find Jacob and kill him. Eliphaz, who was only thirteen years old, had brought a crowd of men with him, and they soon caught up to Jacob as he was about to cross the river. Jacob knew that he could not fight so many men. He said to Eliphaz, "Spare my life, take all my worldly goods, my cattle, my gold, my grain, and bring them to your father, he will be satisfied." Eliphaz agreed. He and his men rode off, leaving Jacob with not even the clothes on his back. A sage said that Eliphaz thought, "He will die and the sin will not lie on my head." Jacob had a vision in his sleep of a long ramp on which angels climbed up and down, and from the top, which reached the gate of heaven, God's voice came promising him, in Genesis 28:12, "I, the Lord am the God of Abraham your father and the God of Isaac. The land on which you lie, to you I will give it and to your seed. And your seed shall be like the dust of the earth and you shall burst forth to the west and the east and the north."

Genesis 29: "And Jacob lifted his feet and went on to the land of the Easterners." So Jacob traveled toward Paddan-aram, picking wild berries, sleeping on the ground, and making a pillow out of stones. He did not die. Each day he came closer to Haran.

From high above, on a sheer rock, a black mountain goat with his long curled horns watched the girl's progress along the path.

Perhaps Rachel saw that a lamb had wandered off the path. She could see him walking on his thin legs as if he had a direction, a purpose, as if he were a traveler off to a better place, rather than a skinny little lamb that would soon be ripped apart by a wolf or mauled by a panther. She chased after him and carried him back to the flock.

Imagine that Rachel's skin was dark from days spent with her flock, and her hair was the color of pinecones on the forest floor. Perhaps she grew restless out in the fields with the sheep and she piled stones up into towers or made them into perfect circles.

A sage said that there had been an outbreak of disease among the animals, and the flock was very small, so a mere girl could manage it. As she approached the well she saw that the three other shepherds were already there, waiting for the group to grow large enough so that there were enough of them to pull on the heavy stone that covered the deep well and open it to the sky so the shepherds could go down to the water and draw it up in pitchers for the waiting animals.

A stranger came toward the well from the other side of the hill. Perhaps his hair was long and he tied it off his face with a long blade of grass. He had no bags with him. He had no animals. Perhaps he had a staff made from a fallen branch in his hand. Had he walked from somewhere else? He was unafraid as he approached the well. The shepherds stared at the man. Was he friend or foe? No one laughed, no one turned their back, no one moved toward the well or away from it. The air must have been heavy with unease. Jacob said, Genesis 29:4, "My brothers, where are you from." And they said, "We are from Haran." And he said to them, "Do you know Laban son of Nahor?" And they said. "We know him." And they said to him, "Look, Rachel his daughter is coming with the sheep."

Rachel saw him. Perhaps she turned her eyes away. Who was he and why did he stare at her?

But there was no anger in the man's face. There was no bitterness about his mouth. He was a pleasing stranger. The man walked up to the stone and with his own arms, with his own back, rolled it off the well. A sage said that Jacob removed the stone as easily as a cork is drawn from a bottle. Jacob put down the stone and he picked up a pitcher to bring water to Rachel's flock. Some sages said that as he began to descend the steps of the well the waters rose from the depths to the very top. There was no need to draw it up, and the waters remained high all the twenty years that Jacob lived in Haran.

How could Jacob lift a great stone that required the strength of many men to move? It was said by the sages that he had been divinely endowed with this supernatural strength on leaving the Holy Land. God had caused the same dew to fall on him that would come from the sky that morning in the far future when the Messiah would appear on earth. It wet his shoulders, his hair, his arms. His physical strength became so great that even in combat with angels he was victorious. The sages were quick to point out that God gave Jacob his unusual strength.

When he had rolled back the stone Jacob walked over to Rachel, who was more beautiful than any woman he had ever seen. She was Laban's daughter. She was his destined bride. He was at that moment overcome with great emotion. Perhaps the wonder of creation had come upon him. He understood for a brief second his purpose on earth, Genesis 29:11, "And Jacob kissed Rachel and lifted his voice and wept." She ought to have been frightened. She had not been kissed before, but instead she leaned toward him, unwilling for him to pull away. Perhaps the other shepherds laughed and joked and made crude gestures with their hands. The sages say that Jacob wept because of the jealous murmurings of the other shepherds.

Perhaps the weeping rose from the sadness of his departure from his home, the guilt that weighed on him because of the blessing he had stolen. All this caused his emotions to rise within him, and now he had seen a woman who had filled him with fierce desire and sweet gentleness in equal proportions.

Perhaps he wept from gratitude to God. He wept from relief that his loneliness would not last forever. He wept from exhaustion from his great efforts. Rashi said he wept because he had no great gifts to bring his bride because all he possessed had been taken from him when he fled his brother's rage.

Their kiss was a promise. A promise neither would ever break.

Later Rabbi Samson Raphael Hirsch said Jacob's choice of Rachel based on the her outward appearance is the reason why half the tribes are descended from Leah's children.

Then Jacob told Rachel that he was her father's kin, that he was Rebekah's son.

Perhaps after the sheep drank from the well, waiting until even the smallest lamb had pushed his way to the rim, Rachel turned her flock back toward Laban's house, her home. She walked as fast as she could with the animals at her side. Jacob waited at the well. He knew that Laban would come for him.

Rachel was eager to tell her family that she had met a stranger who said he was the son of her father's sister. She must have wanted to tell her sister, Leah, that she had met a man who had kissed her by the well, and the kiss was a promise that she knew he would keep. The sisters likely told each other everything that passed through their hearts. It is that way with sisters. Likely Leah would hold Rachel by the hand and lead her to their favorite place behind the tent where no one could see them, and they would play games together that no one else understood, and they would fall asleep in the shade of the elm tree one leaning against the other.

Laban listened to Rachel's story and he ran toward the well, and seeing a stranger there embraced him and kissed him and brought him to his home. This is the second time in his life that Laban had run to the well to greet a stranger. The first time was when he met Eliezar, the servant of Abraham, who had come for his sister. Laban's running footsteps echo the story of that marriage. The echos in Genesis are choruses that bind a song together.

Jacob told Laban that he had come from Isaac's house to find his own way. He did not tell him about his brother's fury or the cause for it. He told him that he had been robbed and had lost all his provisions, all his gold. Laban said to him, "Indeed you are my bone and my flesh."

Rachel told Leah that a man, a man named Jacob, had come from Canaan. He was a relative, the son of the long-gone Rebekah, whom the girls had never known.

Leah was a young woman with a face that was not as round, not as soft, not as pleasing as her sister's. Leah had known that she, the eldest sister, was not the beautiful one for as long as she could remember, likely back into the days after Rachel's birth when the midwife and the servants all said, "what a beautiful baby."

Genesis 29:17 says that Leah's eyes were tender, which may have meant that they were red rimmed, they blinked in the sun, they caused her to rub them, or they were sometimes swollen and sometimes running with yellow pus. It may also have meant lusterless.

What was wrong with Leah's eyes? The sages considered this question. Some say that she had a common disease of the dry countries where flies carried illness in their tiny mouths and blindness was often the end result of years of affliction. Others say that she had been destined to marry Esau, the eldest son of Laban's sister. She had gone to the marketplace to find out what she could about Esau and had heard that he was a wild hunter, a hairy man more comfortable with animals than men, who had married women from the Canaanite tribes, who had a harsh temper and had forsaken the God of his father, Isaac, and his grandfather Abraham. It was said that he was a robber as well as an idolater. When she learned that this was the manner of the man she would marry she began to cry, and she cried and cried until her eyes became sore and infected with the dust that poured in. She cried so hard a sage said that her eyelashes fell out.

She may have wept because she knew her sister was destined for Jacob, whom she was told was a mild man who sat in the tents and turned his mind toward God. If this was true then her sister would surpass her in happiness, would be her superior because of her good fortune to marry the good brother instead of the bad. Perhaps her tears were tears of jealousy.

Others say that she had blue eyes, which are the wrong color for a country where the sun beats so strong for so many months of the year, and that her blue eyes became weak from the sun and she could not see well. Others say she was always envious of her little sister, who seemed to be everyone's favorite from the beginning. Leah's jealousy gave her eyes a hard look, an unpleasant look. But this seems unlikely, because we all know that mean and jealous women are not ugly and that good women are not necessarily beautiful, and it seems more sensible to simply say that Leah was not favored by nature and Rachel was given a double blessing.

If the world were fair, beauty would be distributed in equal amounts. Strength, virtue, and intelligence would be common as weeds, and no living person would have an advantage over the other. But if the world were fair we would have no need to tell stories. Fairness is the enemy of the plot. We would have no need to reach out to our Maker. We would sit like so many stones on the bank of a dry brook, and history would be stalled, rendered pointless. In the unfairness of things Rachel was a beauty and Leah was not.

Rachel's beauty and Leah's lack of grace rectifies another common injustice. The older is given the entire inheritance in the world of the fathers. But here the younger was granted by God something that raised her above her older sister. Just as Jacob was given his mother's greater love and was able to steal the blessing, so Rachel was given beauty, and both second children were favored over their elder sibling, or so it appears at this moment in the story.

Should a man of virtue, a good man, a man whose seed will

become the nation, should such a man be so instantly affected by physical beauty? Shouldn't he look beneath the surface at the soul? Maybe. But Jacob didn't. He saw Rachel and he wanted her to be his bride, his life companion. Perhaps it is asking too much of any man to discount a radiant face. And fortunately for the nation Rachel's soul was as fine as her face, very fine.

Jacob arrived at Laban's home with no gifts for a bride, no wealth to display, no proof that he could keep a family, no cattle, no slaves, no friends, no servants. Laban offered him hospitality, but Jacob immediately went to work in the fields. He was a shepherd. He knew how to care for sheep and camels, goats and donkeys. He was strong and able, and he worked from sunup until sunset for his food and his bed. After a month Laban said to him, Genesis 29:15, "Because you are my kin, should you work for me for nothing? Tell me what your wages should be." Genesis 29:19 says, "Jacob loved Rachel. And he said, 'I will serve seven years for Rachel your younger daughter.' And Laban said, 'Better I should give her to you than give her to another man. Stay with me.' "

What would the world be without tricksters? The first and by far the most evil was the snake in the garden. The second was Abraham, who was pressed by circumstance to fool the pharaoh, and the third was Isaac, who under the same threat played the same game, and the fourth was Jacob, who was urged and aided by his mother our Matriarch to trick Isaac and steal Esau's blessing, and the fifth is making his plans.

Seven is the number of the days of the week, including the six days that it took God to create the world and the seventh day on which he rested. Seven years went by, summer heat, fall chill, winter, and spring. The sun rose and set. Laban's flock grew because of Jacob's care. The flocks increased in numbers and the wealth of the family grew. Perhaps for all those seven years Jacob went to sleep at night thinking of Rachel, whose voice he heard during the day, coming from one place or another, who waved to him in the morning as he left with her father for the fields, who was there in the evening when the family ate their supper, who served him his food but did not sit near him. Perhaps he learned her smell and could tell when she was behind him. Perhaps he learned the songs she liked to sing to herself when she worked. Possibly at night in the moonlight he would walk by her tent and hope she would wake and join him.

Inside her tent she may have heard him pacing the ground outside and recognized his footsteps. It may have seemed to both Rachel and Jacob as if time had stopped moving at all.

And at last it was nearly over, this long wait. Leah, who had at first tried to pretend that nothing had changed between the sisters, must now have become increasingly sad. When Rachel married all would be different. They would no longer share the same tent. No longer would they brush each other's hair and braid it and tie it with cloth. No longer would they go down to the river and chase small silver fish as they darted between their feet.

Leah may have been listless and fallen asleep standing or sitting during the day when they were mending the blankets or removing the pits of the olives. Rachel may have added Leah's share of the work to her own without complaint. When Leah stood, her shoulders must have been hunched over and her narrow face grew even narrower. She must have refused to help Rachel sew the blankets for her wedding bed. She would not help Rachel dye the scarf she would wear on her head or the veil she would wear on her face as she approached her groom.

I am the one he loves, Rachel's heart may have sung, but it must have had the discretion to do so silently. Legend tells us that Rachel could not rejoice when her sister was so without hope. It was as if a great shadow followed her about.

Rachel must not have been able to imagine a world without Leah, a Leah she had known always, a Leah who now would not smile, would not sing, would hardly move from dawn until dusk. When the meal was cooked and the sisters sat at the cloth they had spread before their tent and the servant brought them their lamb, their bread, their olives and chickpeas, Rachel would likely reach forward and eagerly take her portion while Leah would sit still as a rabbit sensing a wolf's approach and would not eat. She must have become thin as the first moon. She must have been tired all the time.

Rachel loved Jacob, but she also loved Leah, and Leah's pain must have spilled over into Rachel's corner of the tent and stained everything.

*L*egend tells us that Laban had teraphim, in his tent. He consulted with them on his plans. The teraphim were small idols made of stone, all except one, his most precious one. This was an oracular idol. If Laban listened closely he thought it spoke to him, in low murmurs, in moans, it revealed the future and gave him guidance. This teraph was made from the head of a slave's firstborn son. Laban had killed the infant as soon as he emerged from the womb. His tiny head was severed from his body and preserved in brine oil and spices. A special coin, a demon coin, was placed under his tongue. It was the custom of the tribes to carry their oracular head with them into wars, to light oil lamps and prostrate themselves before the head and ask it questions. The box in which the head rested was decorated with gold and silver ornaments. Late at night when all were asleep, even the animals drowsing on their feet, Laban asked the oracle if his plan was a good one. The oracle said what it said and Laban felt certain that God would protect him.

The slave woman who never held her son in her arms is nameless. The infant boy is nameless. What we know is that slaves were taken in raids, in tribal wars, from the tents of the defeated whose wives and children could spend the rest of their days in bondage with no hope of release. The woman who bore the infant whose head became the teraph that Laban used had no way to speak of her loss. But surely it was there. After nine months of pregnancy, even if the father was an enemy, her enslaver, she gives birth in the usual pain and blood and then sees, perhaps only for a second, only out of the corner of her eye, the baby, covered in a yellow waxy substance, blood on his limbs, his hair wet. And then she sees the midwife put a pillow over the baby, whose tiny cry stops. She sees the man come with his sword and cut the head from the body of her child. Or perhaps she only hears the blow, the talk of the women around her. How she feels, how she weeps, how she hurts, years afterward, when the same season comes along, all goes unrecorded. But perhaps God knows, God hears. Perhaps He despairs of His creation.

Even He cannot comfort the slave woman, so enormous is her sorrow.

However, over a long time the words spoken to Abraham, to Isaac and to Jacob, were words that overcame the power of the local gods and goddesses and demon figures. The moral might of one great God who reigned over all, who cared for all, warrior and captive alike, who made a covenant with His people to protect them and build them into a great nation, became apparent. It was good that this God did not require the actual sacrifice of human children. The moral power of this great vision has lasted through the roll and the heave of history.

The legends tell us this story: Rachel was out in the fields gathering long grasses to weave into mats for the floor of the tent. The sun was hot on her cheeks and her arms were wet from the warmth of the rays and her own movements up and down. She paused to wipe the drops off her forehead and looked up. There was Jacob. He was standing under a tree, leaning his back against the trunk. He had come to find her. For the first time he told her the true story of his departure from home. He had tricked his father into giving him the blessing that belonged to his brother.

He told Rachel that he believed that Laban would trick him too, fool him by giving him the wrong bride on his wedding night.

Rachel could not believe such a thing of her father. But Jacob insisted. He taught her signs so that he might recognize her under her heavy veils. He begged her to learn the signs. She did as he asked.

Certainly Jacob must have wanted to bring Rachel into his arms. As a man capable of deceit he recognized another who was equally capable. He asked her to remember these private signs. He asked her to touch the great toe of his right foot and then his right thumb and then his right earlobe. Legend tells us that he said to her, "If you do those three things I will know it is you."

Rachel, who had grown up tended by servants, whose mother may have died before Rachel could walk, did not believe her father would harm her. Fathers do not harm their children, she must have believed. Rachel may have wished that Jacob would respect her father as she did.

Jacob had worked well for Laban for seven years and been paid no wages beyond his food. During this time Laban had prospered. The flocks had survived a bad winter. They had increased in number. Several camels must have been purchased and repairs made on the tents. The fields were tilled by the servants, and the cattle were milked and content. Laban found the arrangement with Jacob to his advantage. He considered the matter carefully and made a plan.

As the time for the marriage night approached he called both his daughters into his tent. He told them of his plan to substitute the older sister for the younger under the cover of the bridal veils. Now it must have been Rachel who cried. He did not ask permission. He did not allow his daughters to speak. He told them that they must do as he commanded. Leah must have been ashamed. It was a trick. A trick her future husband might never forgive her for. For the rest of her life her husband would despise her and regret that she was not her sister. This marriage would not end her sorrow. This marriage would not make her beautiful like her sister. She would be an object of scorn. Everyone would know that Leah had been married in the dark, a turtle where a dove should stand.

Rachel heard her father's command and a great despair must have filled her soul. She would have remembered Jacob's kiss and the promise that had come with it, and she was astonished. Could God have forgotten her, could she be thrown down like that, a fall leaf crushed beneath the bear's foot?

She remembered the signs that Jacob had taught her. If Leah did not know the signs then Jacob would suspect that he had been tricked and he would lift the veil and take Leah into the light and see who she was and demand his rightful bride, his chosen one, Rachel. Rachel may not have said a word, not even to her maidservant. She kept her secret and thought about it morning, noon, and night. Toe, thumb, earlobe, right side, she may have said to herself again and again.

Did Rachel think it unfair that she herself could be passed

to a man without her will or kept from that man if she wished to go? Did Leah think it unfair of her father to select her instead of Rachel as his offering to Jacob? Unlikely. The two sisters, like their bondswomen, like the slaves who worked the fields, could not have imagined a world without a heaven above and an earth beneath, so they could not have wished for a freedom they couldn't imagine. The snow goose cannot consider if his life would be better if only his feathers were blue. So too Rachel and Leah assumed that they were of more importance to Laban than his camels, but only as long as they were worth more in profits.

So it must have taken great courage for Rachel to keep the signals that Jacob had given her a secret from her father.

Jacob in the far grass was watching the sheep. He must have been content as he walked about pushing the lambs back into the fold. It was true he had no fortune, that his father's blessing had brought him no gold, but it was also true that he would now have his heart's desire, his beloved, his Rachel, whose soul was good, whose voice was soothing, whose eyes looked on him with affection. His father had said, Marry a woman from your mother's family, and he was doing so. His spirits must have been lifted. He must have thanked God for His everlasting kindness. He thanked his father for his blessing because his marriage to Rachel would be the beginning of his good fortune. How could it not, when his love for her was so strong?

Rachel may have heard the mating song of birds and grieved.

Jacob would scorn Leah, and she would be shamed. Her father would soon be embarrassed before all the assembled. Leah would be mocked. All the wedding guests from the surrounding families would see that Jacob preferred Rachel, the beautiful Rachel. How could Leah live after that? She might ride off on a donkey and die in the forest. How could Rachel let this happen to her sister? Rachel could do this for love of Jacob. She could do it to spite her father who cared not at all for her happiness. But legend tells us she couldn't.

Think of Leah thrust out of Jacob's tent as he called to the world to witness the fraud, just as the encampment would be settling down, the feast dishes carried off, only a few servants wiping tumblers, only a few camels snorting in the air. Leah would stand there in her bridal dress and the veil would be pulled down and her unlovely eyes would be filled with tears.

And here is the moment when Rachel became not just a girl, not just a beautiful girl, but a woman whose words could touch the heart of God when the time came.

Legend tells us that Rachel acted. She may have waited until Leah was asleep, and the only lights for miles around came from the low hanging star that could be seen on the horizon. Laban slept alone, his sword by his side. Jacob slept alone. The two bondswomen that Laban would give to Rachel and Leah slept together wrapped in one blanket. They were Zilpah and Bilhah, the daughters of Laban's concubines. Rachel rose from her pallet and whispered in Leah's ear. Leah turned away from her sister. Leah's sleep was deep. At last she woke.

Rachel told her the signs that Jacob had taught her so he would be sure that she was the bride beside him under the thick veils. She told her sister to touch Jacob's right ear, his right toe, and his right thumb. Leah turned her head away from her sister. It is likely that she was as angry as she was grateful. She was shamed. She knew these signals were a great gift, a sacrifice that her sister had made, and she also knew that it changed nothing. She was still the unwanted bride.

Legend tells us that Jacob deserved this betrayal because of the way he agreed to deceive his father. Perhaps Rachel herself deserved to lose her husband because beauty is not character, and she had not yet proved herself to be worthy of God's love. She was still a girl who may have thought too much of herself.

*M*any centuries later in the small towns of Poland and the Ukraine and across the sprawl of the exile, Jewish brides touched their new husbands on the toe and the thumb and the ear. In the sixteenth century Abraham Azular wrote that this ritual was proper for every bride and groom on their wedding night. He claimed that this touching would arouse the man's desire for honest procreation and drive away demons that incite human lust. If the couple is especially fortunate, he said the bride might give birth to a son already circumcised in the womb.

It was said the priests in the Temple days would put the blood of a sacrificed animal on the earlobe, the big toe, the thumb of their right hand in order to rid themselves of any impurity. There was then something holy in the signs that Jacob gave to Rachel and Rachel gave to Leah. In later times the sages said God granted Rachel a reward for this sisterly kindness: Samson, Joshua, and King Saul were her descendants.

*R*achel did not fall asleep. The thing she had done had been done out of love for her sister, but she had lost her husband, and she knew that she would never again be as light as a cool breeze. She was now just another woman who would go through her days, one after another, because there was no choice.

Leah did not fall asleep either.

The following afternoon as the heat of the day faded, camels appeared on the hill. Here were the other families of Haran invited for the wedding feast. A big pit was dug and goats and a deer were roasted. From flasks made of cow udders wine was poured. Laban went to the other men who had gathered there and spoke to them. Legend tells us that he told them that he had a plan to get Jacob to work for him for seven more years. This pleased the men. Before Jacob had arrived water was scarce, and after he had lifted the stone from the well water flowed easily and rose to the top. They agreed with Laban that his plan was a good one and they would play their part by keeping the secret, by staying late into the night so that it would be dark when Jacob, who would have had much to drink, would enter the marriage tent. Leah would be dressed in her bridal robes. Her hair tied behind her head. The women would have brought her trinkets, little stones, a pressed iris, a piece of mica found on a high rock. Rachel would come and kiss her sister, whose face was not smiling. And Rachel would not smile at Leah.

After the night, after he penetrated her, then she would be his in marriage, his for the rest of his life. He drank perhaps more than he should, but it was a time to celebrate, to dance with the men around the fire, to embrace his father-in-law, for whom he had worked seven long years for no wages. The moon rose high in the sky. The visitors left, singing songs, carrying sleeping children.

Laban had given Zilpah his slave girl to Leah. As Laban fell into a drunken sleep in the arms of one of his concubines, Jacob took Leah, whom he thought was Rachel, to his tent. She was veiled in a heavy cloth—he could not see her face. He was uneasy. He called her name. Rachel, is it you? Leah answered in Rachel's voice, "Yes, I am Rachel." She reached out a hand and touched his right ear. She bent down and touched his right toe. She pulled his hand toward hers and touched his right thumb. These were the signs he had given Rachel. It was Rachel. Jacob lay down content and pulled his bride toward him.

She was careful through the love that followed never to allow the veil on her head to slip. His hands were tender. His words were sweet. He called her Rachel over and over again and each time he did so she was cut to the quick, but she did not stop him. She did not take off her veil. Legend tells us that again and again he called out, "Rachel are you there?" And Leah answered "Here I am."

Rachel alone for the first time in her life in her tent without her sister must have imagined Jacob with his arms around Leah. She must have been wrapped in regret.

For men there is war, there is conquest, there is the pleasure of success at the increase of the healthy herd, at the ripeness of the harvest, at the gaining of land, the winning of gold. For women there is only marriage and children. For women, the ever after begins most often when they are very young, and the sacred book that tells our great adventures barely pauses over a woman's sorrow, hardly more than they would over a sheep trapped in the bramble on a mountain pass. Those things happen but are not the heart of the story, or are they?

As the sky began to grow light Jacob stretched his arms and felt his wife beside him. He had closed his eyes, exhausted, when it was still dark, and now he stirred. Leah sat up in bed. Her veil may have fallen on the rug. The pale light of morning shone through the tent flaps. Jacob must have jumped to his feet and pulled the flaps farther apart and turned to look at his wife. Leah instead of Rachel. Laban had tricked him. Rachel had betrayed him. He must have howled in pain.

For seven years he had worked for Rachel, and look here, before him was Leah. He had not hated her until this moment. But now he must have loathed her. He had touched her body but had thought she was someone else. The sages say that Jacob roared at Leah, "Deceiver, daughter of a deceiver." Anger made him wild, and he flung his arms out as if to hit Leah and then he changed his mind. It was Laban who had done this. He went to Laban's tent. Laban was not there. He was, despite the nights festivities, out among his goats. Jacob followed him there.

Jacob said to Laban, in Genesis 29:25, " 'What is this you have done to me? Was it not for Rachel that I served you and why have you deceived me?' And Laban said, 'It is not done thus in our place, to give the younger girl before the firstborn.

Finish out the bridal week of this one and we shall give you the other as well for the service you render for still another seven years.' And so Jacob did."

How strange it is for a father to refer to his daughters as "this one" or "the other," without names, especially when he is selling them in return for the labor he will receive. It's as if he were referring to the brown goat and the black one: the elderberry tree and the rosebush, his right shoe and his left shoe. But so was the world arranged. And that was why the nation of Israel itself was referred to so often as "she." Israel was small and powerless in a world of large armies, rapists, and marauders. Israel was "she" and "her" and sometimes, "my beloved."

Jacob agreed to Laban's terms. Even today poor Arab villagers still often serve a future father-in-law instead of paying a bride price, and Jacob furnishes them with an honorable precedent.

Perhaps Leah was weeping in the tent of her husband. Her bondswomen Zilpah was trying to comfort her, bringing her oranges and urging her to dry her eyes. Rachel came to the tent. She saw her sister in tears. Her sister who had spent the night where she herself should have been. She may have wanted to sit next to Leah. She may have wanted Leah as her friend. But she must also have seen her now as a rival, the one who took her husband, the one who had enjoyed him in her place, when her body yearned for him, Leah had taken him.

Perhaps Rachel looked at Leah and no words of comfort

passed her lips. She did not sit down but turned her back and walked away. Perhaps Leah put her head down on the bed.

Perhaps the servants were cleaning up the remains of the wedding feast. Rachel was standing among her goats, calling out to them, for each she had a name. They came to her and rubbed against her legs. Perhaps when Jacob's anger subsided he went to find her. Jacob the betrayer must have forgiven Rachel, who betrayed him.

He saw that she was perhaps closer to God than he was, even though God had spoken to him and made him promises. He loved her more than ever because she had not betrayed Leah. He did not embrace her then, but later he would, and he would hold her dear as long as their lives together lasted.

He told her that in a week, after his bridal week with Leah, he would take her as his second wife. He would work for her father another seven years for her sake.

Rachel and Jacob knew that at the end of the seven years they would own nothing, not a sheep nor a goat, nor a camel.

At the end of the week another tent was pitched and another feast was thrown. This time only a few of the neighbors came. This time the musicians only played for a little while. Leah sat alone with her bondswoman and stared at the plate of food before her. The sadness in her face would not have made her more beautiful. During the evening Rachel may have looked at her sister. She might have pitied her. Laban gave his own slave girl Bilhah to Rachel.

That night in the dark Jacob must have removed Rachel's veil. He would have needed to see her face, the face that he had wanted since he had first seen it at the well seven years before. In joy they must have spent the night.

Leah must have been alone in her tent. Zilpah may have slept outside, listening to the sound of a wolf on the hill as it called to its mate. The moon rose on Leah's tent, and she must have lamented, and the moon turned white and fell into the morning sky and Leah still lamented.

*M*arriage to two sisters is prohibited in Leviticus. After the sixth century B.C.E. marriage to two sisters was strictly forbidden. In many ways the makers of the law, the sages and rabbis, tried to make a woman's lot easier. They knew that the feminine was part of God, and God's purpose could not be fulfilled without women. The sages spoke of the Shekinah, the female aspect of God's being, that broke into a myriad number of tiny fragments when Adam and Eve left the Garden and their way of return was blocked by angels with flaming swords. Those tiny fragments must be woven into a whole before the Messiah will come. When a woman weeps, those fragments will splinter once again into even tinier pieces, making the task of repair just that much harder.

*J*acob began his second seven years of servitude to Laban with two wives. One he loved. The other he did not. Each time he looked at Leah he must have been reminded that he had been tricked, that she had lied to him. "I am Rachel," she had said. Each time he looked at her he must have felt angry that he

had worked so many days and so many nights and been rewarded only with a woman he did not want. But he was a man
of honor, and a man of honor has an obligation to his wife. He
could avoid speaking to her as much as possible. He could
sleep in the tent with Rachel most of the time, but he had an
obligation as Leah's husband to visit her at night once in a
while. It would not be right to do otherwise.

She would have smiled when she saw him lift the tent flap
and approach her. She would have hoped that in time he might
learn to love her or at least accept her without regret. Surely
she soaked her body in aromatic oils. She brushed her hair a
thousand times. She would have learned a new song from her
slave girl that she sang to him. She would have made sure he
had wine by his bedside. She must have stroked his hand gently
and turned her head away from him so he wouldn't have to
look at her imperfect eyes. But likely he would come to her and
tell her to lie down and he would take her body and not touch
her tenderly. He would not have called her sweet names. He
would not stay and speak of the happenings of his day. He
would have taken her as he was bound to do, and as infre-
quently as was decent.

But his body had awakened her body, and she must have
yearned for him, becoming joyous when he appeared at her
side. By the custom of the time and the place, she would never
have another man by her side as long as she lived. Because he
had taken her on their wedding night she was his property and
no other would have her, no other would take pity on her, no
other would desire her. When he left her tent without a word
she must have been even more alone than before he had come.

Genesis 29:31 says, "And the Lord saw that Leah was despised." It says in Genesis Rabbah that "all hated her. Sea travelers abused her, land travelers abused her saying this Leah leads a double life: she pretends to be righteous but is not for if she were so righteous would she have betrayed her sister?"

Rachel too saw that Leah was despised. She grieved for her sister. But she must have been pleased for herself. Both emotions warred within her. One must have won out over the other and then succumbed to the power of its opposite. Perhaps Rachel's beauty had never been more astonishing. Her face glowed with the happiness of her husband's love. Leah had never been more sallow. Her long features may have grown longer. Her eyes may have been even more infected. She did not eat well. She did not sleep well, and through the long hours of the night when the cattle were dreaming she may have paced about, disturbing Zilpah, her bondswoman, in her restless meanderings.

Worst of all she would not have been able to tell Rachel of her hurt. Rachel to whom she likely had always told everything that flowed through her mind. Rachel, who had seemed to her a part of herself, more than a friend, a refuge, now was far away from her no matter how near she was in fact. It would hurt Rachel to know how Leah grieved, and Leah may well have been happy for her sister, even in her own despair. Also less noble but of equal importance, she may not have wanted to give Rachel reasons to feel even more superior to her than she already did. Silence may then have become her habit.

Leah may have turned away when her sister came near with an offer to join her for a meal, to go for a walk the way they had before their marriages.

Some might say that the sisters should have stood together and demanded equal love and attention from their husband. Some might think that if Rachel had been generous and Leah had been patient Jacob would have learned to love each of his wives. But Jacob did not love Leah. And then there is the matter of possession. Each of the sisters likely wanted the exclusive love of a husband. It may be the custom of the land that a man may have many wives, but that custom clearly favors the male inclination, leaving women to hold their tongues, to wake at night and hear sounds that infuriate, sounds that diminish. Possession of another human being is perhaps not the noblest of desires. But it was more than Rachel and Leah could do, to share equally a man, especially a man who preferred Rachel to her sister.

Leah was envious of her sister. Envy is not new to this story. Cain was envious of the love that God gave to Abel, and when he could not win that love for himself he killed Abel. Satan was envious of the Lord himself and came down to Eden to spoil God's Garden. Envy has toppled kings and caused queens to lose their heads, and it knocks around in the walls of holy sees and palaces and parliaments and subcommittee meetings of petty bureaucrats and hospital administrators, and it even poisons the coffee of artists and poets, scholars and athletes. No surgeon can remove it from the human soul.

Rachel and Leah may have wished each other harm. Those were just wishes, sparks that envy creates.

*G*enesis 29:31 says, "And the Lord saw that Leah was despised and he opened her womb but Rachel was barren." Rabbi Judah b. Simon, Rabbi Simon, and Rabbi Hana said in the name of Rabbi Samuel b. and Rabbi Isaac, "When the Patriarch Jacob saw how Leah deceived him by pretending to be her sister he determined to divorce her but as soon as the Holy One Blessed Be He visited her with children, he exclaimed shall I divorce the mother of these children?"

For many months Rachel must have seen the child growing inside of Leah. Leah would now have taken food. Her color would have returned to her cheeks. Her hair must have been combed with care. Rachel saw that Leah had overtaken her by conceiving a child. It will happen to me too, soon, Rachel must have believed. But it didn't.

Rachel did not conceive even though Jacob spent many more nights with her than he spent with Leah.

And Leah's time came. Her servant Zilpah ran and called the midwife. Perhaps Leah was placed on a rug on the ground under the stars and the moon. Her pains were not unusual, her courage was great. She may have called for Rachel in the last moments, but Rachel, who had just started another time of bleeding, hid her head in her cushions. Jacob must have stood outside of Leah's tent. This women he did not love was doing well. She was like the ewes in the flock increasing his lot, bringing him the most valued of possessions, a future that would live past his own death. Likely he was not this night angry with her for her trick.

He could see that God favored him, would fulfill His promise to him, making him the father of generations, a father of nations. As he waited a decent distance from the birthing, away from the coming and going of females, he must have thanked God for his good fortune.

The stars moved across the sky as they always did. The hand of God was presumed to be everywhere, guiding the infant down the birth canal, holding the woman's hand as she cried into the wind. The midwife soothed and patted, talked and walked about, and Leah must have endured the pain that returned and returned, receded and left her sweating on her bed, blinking in the near dark, looking for rescue, longing to be held. The midwife must have whispered encouragement. Outside Jacob waited. Across the wide field Laban waited too. In her tent, Rachel must have tried to sleep but could not. She would not have gone to her sister's side. She must have waited for Jacob to come to her, but he did not.

Leah would now have pushed the baby out of her body. The head appeared, and the midwife pulled the infant out, and the baby cried out and was heard by all those who had gathered around. Jacob might have howled in triumph. Laban might have hugged his concubine and pinched her in joy. The midwife would have come out to tell everyone, a boy, a healthy boy.

And what if the baby had been a girl? That question does not belong in this book.

෯

*L*eah must have held her son. She smiled at him. Genesis 29:32, "—and called his name Reuben, for she said, 'Yes, the Lord has seen my suffering, for now my husband will love me.'" The word *Reuben* in Hebrew can mean "see, a son." In the notes by Robert Alter in his translation of Genesis he suggests that Leah converted the word into a verb, making God see her pain. God may have known how Leah was neglected, but He could not or would not change the heart of her husband as it leaned toward Rachel morning, noon, and night and pulled away from Leah despite the birth of the baby, despite Jacob's pleasure in that birth.

After eight days the baby was circumcised. Leah's people were pledged to a God who had asked this of them and so it would be. The tiny baby would be cut and his foreskin removed and ever after he would be marked as one of theirs. Leah must have thought of the baby's pain. She must have changed the small cloth they had placed on him. She put on the oils they had given her. Leah let her baby look at her face, and he did not find her ugly.

Leah must have brought her baby to her breast and felt the flow of milk into his mouth and watched each day as his eyes opened wider and he grew to recognize her face. She saw that he called for her in hunger and welcomed her arms with joy. She had seen the cord that the midwife had cut at his birth and the cord remained in her mind, a tie that would be there ever after. The hunch in her shoulders left her. Her skin became rosy. The baby yearned for her. Never before had she been necessary.

Now she was the equal of her sister, if not in grace than in fortune. She must have wanted to show the baby to Rachel, to have her admire his small feet, the crevices in his thighs, the slope of his nose, the tufts of hair that stood out on his head. But Rachel likely would not come to her.

It must have been clear that when Jacob returned to visit Leah's tent he was doing so in hopes of having another son, not because he wished to be in her arms. But perhaps for Reuben's sake he was less harsh with her, less abrupt, allowing her time to lie beside him. His anger with her was surely abating, cooling, leaving in its place a space where hatred might become indifference. And Leah conceived again.

*R*achel was still barren. Like Sarah and Rebekah she must have waited and yearned and longed for and suffered disappointment over and over again. She was still beautiful. Standing on a mound outside of the tents Jacob might have seen her when he sat out to tend the ever growing flock. But into her eyes a new sadness appeared. Without a child she was like a dry river unvisited by man or beast, empty of fish.

She saw Leah with Reuben and Leah now full again with another child, and she must have wondered, What had she done to displease the Lord?

Reuben was barely able to walk when Leah's time came again. Now she knew what to expect. She must have again prayed to the Lord to help her through. She held the hand of Zilpah, and her fingernails dug deep into the palms of her servant, who didn't complain. But the birth was easier, faster, and it seemed as if an angel were helping the baby down the birth canal, so eager was he to arrive in the world. His first cry was lusty and full and Rachel may have heard it outside the tent and her eyes filled with tears. These would not have been simple tears of envy. She and Leah had been everything to each other for a long time before Jacob had come to Haran, and a birth was a birth, always a matter of wonder, bringing tears into anybody's eyes.

The afterbirth slid onto the blanket and the baby was washed in a great bowl and Jacob must have come and seen his son and he was pleased, a second son, God had been good to him. Jacob saw Leah lying on the pallet with the baby on her chest. Jacob's sons were part of God's promise. But it's probable that Jacob didn't touch Leah. He didn't look in her face. He didn't sit beside her. He spent less time with her than with a ewe who had birthed triplets. Leah would have closed her tender eyes. She would have been exhausted from the birth, and she must have known that Jacob had not changed toward her.

Genesis 29:34 says, "And she said, 'Yes, the Lord has heard I was despised and He has given me this one, too,' and she called his name Simeon." Simeon has as a root the word *shma*, meaning "hear." The notes to Robert Alter's translation of Genesis say that Jacob's first two sons are named after sight and sound, the two senses that might have revealed Jacob's deception of his father, Isaac. If Isaac had listened more carefully he would have known the voice claiming to be Esau's was

Jacob's, and if he had been able to see his son Jacob in Esau's clothes he might have prevented the deception.

It seems, however, more likely that Leah named her sons for the two senses by which she felt abused. Jacob did not like to look at her, and Jacob did not like to hear her. She felt erased and silenced when she so dearly needed him to recognize her, to hear her. Since the right to name the infant was Leah's she sent a coded plea to her husband through her choice of her sons' names: see me, hear me!

*P*erhaps Jacob left Leah with his sons by her side to celebrate with the men. And when the time came to fall asleep he must have returned to Rachel's tent. She would have opened her arms to him as he wrapped himself in her body. This was where he slept peacefully. This was where he needed to be. The other wife could give him a hundred sons but the only one he loved, the only one he wanted, was Rachel.

Leah was in her tent with her second baby on her breast, the first baby sleeping by her feet, the warmth of new life all over her, and she was still without.

*A*nd out in the fields Jacob worked for no wages, through heat and burning sun, through dust storms that made him wrap his face in his head cloth and wipe his tearing eyes again and again. He watched the men sow the fields with barley seed. He helped pick the olives that would be pressed into oil, oil for cooking, oil for dipping bread, olives for their sour juices eaten at the end of the day with wine. He tracked his goats, protecting them from foxes, wisely removing them from places where he saw the prints of the wolf embedded in the dirt. He listened to the sound of the wind and knew which direction to move to avoid the worst of a sandstorm. Sometimes he was gone for days as he crossed the valley and then climbed the far hills to find grass that had not browned in the scorching sun.

It is likely that more than once he heard the sounds of approaching camels as he and his men were resting in the shade of a tree and that he heard the whistles of men as they signaled one another. He heard their feet on the ground and took up his sword and moved forward. He was not a man who liked to draw another man's blood. He was not eager to slash and bruise and to kill another human being, even one who would kill him without hesitation. Jacob must have known that God had not created man so that he could slaughter his fellow man. But when the occasion arose, Jacob was not slow to move, to show the would-be robbers, the pirates of the field, that the goats that belonged to Laban would stay with Laban, the lives of his men would not be taken, the goblets and vessels, the wine and the water they carried with them, would stay with them, and the robbers and the killers would retreat, sometimes carrying their wounded or their dead with them. That is the way it was in that part of the world at that time.

And Leah conceived again. And still Rachel did not. The months passed quickly as Leah played with Reuben, and nursed Simeon, and taught Reuben to dip his bread in the chickpeas, and taught him the words for all the birds in the trees, and together they picked figs from the branches. She carried Reuben on her back and Simeon in a sling around her waist and walked to the well to show them the water rising high, the water that came with his father, because of his father.

Leah's time came again. Would all go well? Would the baby be born alive? Would the mother survive? These questions attended every birth. The danger was real. Disaster was always possible. This is why the faces of those who helped Leah were white with fear. This is why the men stayed far away, as if they could keep catastrophe away from their bodies by staying at a distance. Leah, however, labored only a short time and she laughed at the end when she saw that she had given birth to another son. She said, Genesis 29:34, "This time my husband will join me, for I have born him three sons." She named the baby Levi. The name Levi plays on the word *yilaveh*, meaning "will join." Despite her earlier disappointment Leah still hoped that the birth of this son would turn Jacob's heart toward her. Perhaps the baby had beautiful dark eyes and his limbs were perfect. Jacob would have been pleased by its form. Laban would have embraced his son-in-law. Rachel would have wept out of bitterness in her tent.

*L*egend tells us that Jacob did not move his possessions out of Rachel's tent. Likely he was no longer angry at Leah, but he did not love her, not even after three sons. Her hopes proved false.

Yet now she had her babies, and they clung to her side,

they called her name, they suckled at her breast. They, after all, had no choice, no other mother tempted them to turn their heads away from her. Leah must surely have yearned for her sister, the only other person on earth who might understand and comfort her, if she were not her enemy, her victorious rival.

Now when Jacob entered her tent she must have known that there was no point in pouring oils on her body. She would not tie up her hair or wear her favorite red robe. She would not speak to him or attempt to caress him. It was another child he wanted and that was all. She conceived again and bore him another son. She did not name him as she had the others. Genesis 29:35 says "She conceived again and bore a son, and she said, 'This time I sing praise to the Lord,' therefore she called his name Judah."

And now there must have been endless commotion around her. The boys would have jumped and yelled and punched one another, sometimes in anger, sometimes in play. They grew stronger with each week. As soon as they were able they would have gone out to the fields and helped as long as they could with the work. They went to the stream and splashed and threw rocks. Everyone in the camp, Laban too, would have smiled at them as they passed by. Everyone in the camp, Rachel too, would have saved them a fine bunch of grapes as a treat. When they met Rachel on the path she looked at them as if each child were a miracle. When they left her presence she was bitten by envy. Their calls to one another, their small boy arms waving, their clear voices put salt in her wounds, but also gave her pleasure. Children of her husband, children of her sister, like the trees in the forest nearby, like the water in the well, like the goats and the camels and the bushes ripe with berries, they were part of her place too. Genesis Rabbah explains that Rachel envied the extent of Leah's good deeds, reasoning, "Were she not righteous would she have borne children?" There is a rabbinic principle that all deeds are repaid in kind, so Jacob's tricking of Isaac was repaid with Laban's tricking Jacob, and therefore Leah's good deads were repaid with children and Rachel's assumed lack of virtue repaid with a barren womb.

*I*f only it were true that the righteous were rewarded and those without virtue punished, but the world we know is not so orderly. Happiness is rare and justice uncertain.

*I*n the early hours of the morning when Jacob had woken with the piercing call of a bird and taken Rachel in his arms and afterward they had lain together awake she may have complained to him that he had sufficient sons and asked him to stop visiting Leah. Likely he made no promise to Rachel, but legend tells us that he stayed away from Leah for a long time and she waited for him night after night in vain.

Some months passed. Perhaps Jacob spent time alone with neither of his wives. His body was restless. He may have thanked the Lord for all the sons that he had, but he wanted more sons. He wanted more the way he wanted the flock to keep increasing, the bush by the tent to grow more buds, the rain to rain harder. And Rachel, who loved him, must have seen his restlessness.

Each day, she saw Leah walking about with her sons, one still a baby on her arm. She must have gone to visit Leah, pretending to admire the children, speaking sweetly to them, but each moment by their side cut her heart open. And then she must have been ashamed because Leah was her sister, her only sister, and the boys were flesh of her flesh even if they had not been ushered from her womb.

Legend tells us that Rachel was afraid. She was afraid that she would meet the fate of other barren women. She had heard the servants talking. She knew that she could be sent back to Laban and divorced. She had heard Laban's serving girl whispering about Esau. She had heard that her father was planning on sending her to Esau to marry. Esau would have her because she was his cousin, and since he had many other wives and many children he would take her, a prize despite her inability to bear children. She had heard that Esau had a wild temper and could harm those close to him. She would have to leave Jacob whom she loved. She told herself that Jacob would not send her away, even if she bore him no children. But she could not have been certain. Other men had done just that to their barren wives. Other men returned their wives if they did not produce, the way you would return an animal you had purchased who turned sick on the way home.

Genesis Rabbah says that it is children who preserve a woman's position in the home. No wonder Rachel was afraid of exile. In her fear her anger at her sister grew. The unfairness seemed beyond bearing. She passed Leah at the well, and Leah was with her smallest boys, and Rachel did not greet her. She turned her head away. Leah may have called out to her. But Rachel hurried away.

Perhaps it was when she was sitting with Jacob as he ate his supper that she said to him, in Genesis 30:1, "Give me sons, for if you don't I'm a dead woman." And he became incensed with Rachel, and he said, "Am I instead of God, who has denied you fruit of the womb?" And she must have known that she had shamed herself in his eyes.

God banished chaos and subdued the void and He created life, and each time a woman conceives it is not some stone fertility goddess who has triumphed but the Lord himself who creates the miracle that occurs under the woman's ribs, within her belly.

Genesis 30:3: "And she [Rachel] said, 'Here is my slave girl Bilhah. Come to bed with her that she may give birth on my knees, so that I too, shall be built up through her.'"

At that time, to place a baby on someone's knees was the way an adoption was sealed.

This is the echo of the story of Hagar and Sarah. Sarah too hoped to be granted a son through Hagar, but wasn't, not really. Rachel gave Bilhah to Jacob as a wife, and Bilhah conceived and bore him a son. Rachel said, "God granted my cause, yes he heard my voice and he gave me a son." She called his name Dan and she held the baby and sung to him and kept him by her side, but it is likely that his slave mother told him who his true mother was, and he often turned his head away from Rachel. When he could, he ran to Bilhah, who wrapped him in her shawls and took him off to private places. Rachel must have been pleased with the baby, but she surely knew that he was not hers, not hers to boast of, not hers to bind to, not hers to worry over. He was borrowed, and whenever possible as soon as he was able, he would return to his true mother and Rachel was left once again alone.

Can you imagine Bilhah's eyes as she watched Rachel wash her own infant? A slave is a slave and cannot change the course of events, but she must know pain. There is no way that a slave cannot long for her own flesh and blood, and bitter she must have been the moment she placed him on Rachel's lap.

Now that Bilhah was his, Jacob was content, and Bilhah conceived again. Rachel was not surprised. But surely when Bilhah told her she had conceived again her hands must have trembled as she picked up a pitcher of water to pour into a waiting basin.

Bilhah gave birth to a second son. As recounted in Genesis 30:8, Rachel named the second son. "And Rachel said, 'In awesome grapplings I have grappled with my sister and yes, I won out' and she called his name Naphtali." *Naphtali* contains the word that means *wrestling*. Now Jacob had six sons.

Although Rachel here claims that she has won over her sister she must have known that she had not. She has not given birth herself. Out of the love that she bears Jacob, out of the love he gives to her, nothing has come. She has the possession of Bilhah's two children, but still she must know that in the eyes of the world, in the eyes of the Lord, in Jacob's eyes, she is a barren woman whose womb remains closed, locked, empty.

Now Jacob does not come to Leah's side anymore. But it says in a version of the story that Leah knows a way to reduce her sister's pleasure. She gives her slave girl Zilpah to Jacob, and he accepts the gift with gratitude. Perhaps he even smiles at Leah when she brings the slave to his tent. He looks in Leah's face. The face he had once found so detestable is now a familiar face, a known face, a face that looks on him kindly and has brought him a gift. Zilpah too gives birth to a son, and Leah names the child Gad and says, "Good luck has come." The sages say that Gad was born circumcised, which was possible because the Lord could do anything. If he created man with a foreskin he could surely bring into the world a baby without one. But why this child and not another. Could someone be imagining things for the sake of the story, to make God seem even more beyond compare? It would seem unnecessary to invent stories that made God's presence in the world more apparent. A person has only to open his eyes in the morning and God could be seen everywhere. No need for babies to be born already circumcised. But the theme of the son born circumcised would last through the ages, echoing the piety of mankind and the continual hope for the miraculous.

As soon as the baby was weaned from his mother's breast Zilpah conceived again and bore another son. This one Leah named Asher. Leah said, Genesis 30:11, "What good fortune." "Now," said Leah, "I have six sons." Leah must have taken comfort in the strength of her sons and given them all of her heart because Jacob reserved no portion for himself.

*J*acob does not send Rachel away. Not because her slave girl gave him two sons but because he would never have parted from her. From the first moment he saw her by the well he must have known he would keep her by him whatever the Lord brought to him, no matter how his fortunes turned. His manservants may have urged him to return Rachel to her father. Jacob knew that she brought him no profit, but every night he visited her tent.

Sarah had made Abraham send Hagar into the desert with a child on her back. The first wife has the final say. Would Leah insist that Rachel be sent away? Leah must have known that she could make this request. But she must also have known that it would not be granted. Also she would not have forgotten that her sister had given her the signals that saved her from shame on her wedding night. Perhaps an angel heard Leah and comforted her. Perhaps the Lord heard Leah and sorrowed for her.

*T*he children grew. The sun rose and set and the seasons changed. When it was harvesttime the children joined the others in the fields and brought in baskets of grain, barrels of olives, almonds, and grapes. Jacob worked in the heat and the cold and often slept in the fields, watching his flock.

Reuben was the eldest son, and he dearly loved his mother. He went into the fields with his father's donkey to harvest the barley. He had worked since the first sign of sun in the morning, and now it was nearly noon. Legend tells us that he saw in the gully just a few feet away a mandrake, its round, bloodred fruit oozing juice from a place where an insect had penetrated the soft skin. Its thorny leaves shone in the light. Legend says that the mandrake appeared as if lightning were coming out of its fruit, darting up to the sky. Perhaps he had heard talk about the mandrake; its powers were strange and great. It could cure fevers, heal wounds, and open the wombs of barren women; it could reverse the weakening of age and mend broken bones. It would make a man adore his wife and a woman long for a man. He would bring it to his mother, who pined for the attention of his father. He went to pull it up. It resisted. He tried again with all his strength, and the mandrake plant seemed to pull back, as if it were attempting to bring him down under the earth. Reuben would not give up. He tied a rope around the plant, and he attached the rope to the donkey's saddle. The donkey straining at the ropes could not move forward when he was told. Reuben climbed on his back and hit him with a stick hard and harder, and the donkey moved first one foot and then another. He pulled himself forward despite the mandrake's resistance.

For over an hour the donkey pulled. The mandrake pulled back. Reuben was soaking wet with effort. The donkey was exhausted. A white foam appeared at the sides of its mouth. At last the mandrake seemed to lose heart, and when the donkey stepped forward Reuben eased on the rope. Legend tells us that as the donkey moved forward again and as the plant began to rise from the earth a great scream was heard. The mandrake howled a terrible howl, a shriek of terror, a scream of rage, and then an unholy sound came from the ground, as if the mandrake were sobbing, mourning for itself. It came up from the ground and lay in the field, the rope still attached, and the roots trembling as the two bulbs at its base pulsed up and down and up and down. The cry had been so terrible the donkey had flattened its ears and tried to run away but was hobbled by the weight of the plant. The plant screamed, the donkey frothed at the mouth, and then the donkey sank to its knees and turned on its side and died. It was said that the only way to pull a mandrake out of the ground was to pour a woman's menstrual blood on it, or perhaps her urine. Otherwise the mandrake kills whomever tugs at its roots. It was said that the mandrake had a vengeful spirit. Perhaps.

Robert Graves and Raphael Patai tell us in their footnotes that Pliny had written in his *Natural History* of the danger of quickly uprooting this plant. In the Middle Ages there were reports of the mandrake being used as an anesthetic during surgical operations. One of the Ugaritic texts from the fifteenth or fourteenth century B.C.E. speaks of a fertility cult and begins by saying, "Plant mandrakes in the earth." A millennium and more later Shakespeare wrote in *Romeo and Juliet*:

"And shrieks like Mandrakes torn out of the earth
that living mortals hearing them, run amok."

$\mathcal{S}$hakespeare also lists the mandragora among the drowsy syrups of the East. Graves and Patai suggest that the mandrakes antispasmodic quality may explain why it was thought to cure barrenness, since a woman's muscular tension can prevent conception. There is an ancient Germanic tradition of using the mandrake as part of a prophetic ceremony. The mandrake's prophetic power seems to arise from the wild ramblings of those under its narcotic influence.

And William Blake wrote a poem.

Go, and catch a falling star,
Get with child a mandrake root.

$\mathcal{T}$he mandrake is also called Satan's apple.

$\mathcal{L}$egend says that Reuben waited and watched the plant until it was very still for a long time. Then he went over and cut the rope away. He picked up the plant, and held it in his hands. Now it was just a plant, but a moment before it had been something else. He looked at the two round bulbs at its base, which seemed so much like his own testes. Reuben may have given thanks to God for including the mandrake in His creation.

He may have run back to camp, calling out to all, come see

what I have brought for my mother. Leah, who was picking up figs from the ground beneath the large fig tree in the nearby grove, hurried to see what her son had found. She saw the mandrake and took it in her hands, which were suddenly stained purple. The mandrake has been called "a little man." Leah may have laughed. It was said that the mandrake could cure sores of the breast, aches in the fingers, pain in the head, and make wounds heal in a moment's time. Just then Rachel came.

There was a crowd around the plant. Leah embraced her son. Rachel had heard that the mandrake plant would make its owner full with child. Genesis 30:14–15: "And Rachel said to Leah, 'Give me pray, some of the mandrakes of your son.' And Leah said, 'Is it not enough that you have taken my husband and now would take the mandrakes of my son?' "

Leah stared at her sister and the stare could not have been friendly. The mandrake stayed in Leah's hands. She must have clutched it tightly. The roots were beginning to shrivel up. The bulbs were losing their fullness. Rachel may have been weeping. Was this her last chance?

Rachel said to Leah, Genesis 30:16, "Then let him lie with you tonight in return for the mandrakes of your son." Leah paused. Her body yearned for her husband. Legend hints that because of Rachel's plea to him it had been many seasons since he had come to Leah. Also Leah must have known that she didn't need the mandrake to conceive. If she gave the plant to Rachel she would lose no advantage. She must also have known how her sister ached for a child of her own, out of her own womb. Possibly it was her wish too that Rachel bear a child. Should that happen perhaps she wouldn't praise the child, as Rachel likely had said little good about her own sons, but she might well be thankful to the Lord God who had eased her sister's wound.

Perhaps the two sisters looked at each other, each having what the other wanted, each unable to speak the words that would rekindle the affection that had once been so easy, so natural for them.

And in the evening when the sky was a pale gold Jacob came in from the fields. Two donkeys brayed on the hill. The camels settled down to rest.

Leah, wearing her best robe, bathed and oiled, her hair combed and tied with a grass leaf, a loose scarf over her head, came out to greet him. He would have walked past her but she blocked his way on the path. She said, Genesis 30:16, "With me you will come to bed, for I have clearly hired you with the mandrakes of my son."

Jacob understood that he had been purchased for the price of an ugly plant with great bulbs at its root. A man should not be for hire. A man is not an animal that can be penned with another so it breeds. A man has the right of choice between his wives. His favors should not be paid for.

Several sages said that Rachel never ate the roots of the mandrake, which would have been sorcery, but that she gave them to a priest, and God rewarded her with two sons for having conquered so strong a temptation.

*J*acob was a man who served the one true God. He was the grandson of the man who had first found the Lord, to whom the Lord had made promises that depended on the worthiness of those who followed. Jacob had spoken with the Lord, had seen angels climbing up and down ladders; he had been given promises. Leah stood before him, no longer a frightened young girl, not beautiful like Rachel, but strong and proud and assured, the mother of four of his sons, and as such, a woman deserving of respect. He looked at her eyes, the eyes that were not good, and he saw in them a determination he had not expected. She would not easily be denied.

As she stood there, the sun sinking behind her, the sky turning orange and pink at the horizon's edge, desire rose in his body, as if a single ray of sun had crossed his skin, sunk deep into his muscles, warming him. It had been a long time since he had been with Leah.

And he lay with her that night.

Some say that Rachel knew that one day soon Jacob would want to leave Paddan-aram and leave her father's service for his homeland. She knew that her father would never let her go if she did not give birth to a child. Instead for the sake of a parcel of land Laban would marry her off to a neighbor who worshipped idols. And she would lose everything.

*R*achel spent that night alone in her tent. Legend says she grated the mandrake, she prepared it with milk and the fruit of an orange. She ate the mandrake, roots and all. The bulbs were sour, but she ate them anyway and and hoped and prayed to God, this time to open her womb and do for her what He had done for Sarah and Rebekah in their time. Perhaps she told

God that she would not think evil thoughts about her sister anymore. Perhaps she promised God that she would do His bidding in all things. Perhaps she wept and promised God that if she bore a child she would raise that child to love Him beyond all others.

Surely Leah clasped Jacob to her.

God must have seen Leah's tears when in the first hours of dawn Jacob rose and without saying a word to her, gathered his things and left for the fields.

Probably Leah slept long into the morning and then as the noon sun chased everyone into the shade of a tree, or the coolness of the stream. She lay down on a pallet, hoping a breeze would come down from the mountains. Again she slept. In the early evening perhaps she watched her boys climbing a tree. And then she slept some more. She spent the day thinking about the night that had passed, looking backward, not forward. But as she thought these bittersweet thoughts, deep within her body the miracle of life began.

Leah had conceived.

Leah, of whom Jacob was so careless, was loved by God. Leah would find once again the joy of a young child, sleeping, sucking, clinging to her side. If her husband would not love her, her children would make up for his folly.

Some of the sages, however, criticized Leah for her forwardness, for her lack of modesty, and said that the destruction of the first Temple was the punishment for her brazenness—a punishment suffered by her descendants. Other sages found fault with Rachel, who had acted without first seeking the approval of her husband. Genesis Rabbah castigated Rachel for treating Jacob's devotion casually. They claimed it was for this reason that she was not buried with her husband. Rabbi Simon taught, "Because she slighted that righteous man she died before her time." These particular critical comments rise from the unforgiving culture of the time when they were written and are intended primrily to increase our respect for the nation.

What would have brought Rachel and Leah together again? There is no report of their love for each other in Genesis. The story is not about a sister who lost a sister in their marriages to the same husband. Perhaps they joined together to nurse a sick child. Perhaps they joined each other in the same tent when a sandstorm blew across the land. Perhaps they remembered the times of their childhood and were able to talk again, in friendship. Perhaps not.

Leah gave birth when the time was right. Leah called this son Issachar and said "God has given me my wages," because I gave my slave girl to my husband. And Rachel must no longer have tried to keep Jacob away from Leah's tent, and Leah gave birth to a sixth son, and she called him Zebulun. Leah said, "God has granted me a goodly gift. This time my husband will exalt me for I have born him six sons." It was not true that any number of sons, sons in the thousands, could bring Jacob to love Leah. This is her tragedy and her strength: she kept hoping, surviving disappointment after disappointment.

This futile expectation at the birth of the sixth child must have hung in the air of the camp, caused the oils to burn brightly. The angels in heaven might have sighed. Leah would not be loved, not as Rachel was loved, and Leah would never be content.

And then Leah conceived for the seventh time. Legend tells us that she pitied her barren sister Rachel, and prayed: "O Lord, let this child be a girl, lest my sister Rachel should again grow jealous!" God then changed Leah's child from male to female, and told her: because you pitied your sister Rachel, I will grant her a son. And that is why Dinah was born to Leah and Joseph to Rachel.

Jacob held his daughter in his arms. He prayed to God. Legend tells us that he said, "Let no harm befall her. Let her be like the blossom on the almond tree, beautiful to see, signaling the harvest to come." Perhaps Jacob did something he had never done before, not with the birth of his sons. He may have leaned over his baby and kissed her eyes, a tenderness coming over him causing him to be thankful for life, fearful of its loss.

In another slightly different version of the same story a sage wrote: "Leah said, 'Six sons have issued from me and four from the handmaids making ten, if this child is a male, my sister Rachel will not be equal to the handmaidens.' Forthwith her child who was initially male was turned into a girl." Rachel would be unequal to the handmaidens if Leah had another male because she would not have produced any sons, although she had given Jacob two through her handmaiden and Leah would have given him seven. A daughter does not count in the numbers, nor could she become a tribal leader enhancing the nation. This version tells us about rivalry between females, each with the other over this question of producing male children, which was of enormous consequence at that time. The strength of the group, the way it could increase in later generations, its success in battle, its ability to keep and gather precious goods, depended on male muscle, bravery, courage.

This story tells us that Leah had compassion for her childless sister, just as her sister had shown her when she taught her the signals for the bridal bed.

And Leah named her daughter Dinah, which means "judgment." Some of the rabbis read this birth in another way. They said that Dinah's gender is judgment against Leah for her desire to further humble her sister. Rabbi Abba agreed with those who said that Dinah was turned into a female through Rachel's pleas. On the other hand in M. Berakot it says, "If a man cried over what is past his prayer is in vain. Thus if his wife is pregnant and he says, 'May God grant that my wife bear a male child' this is a vain prayer." Which makes good biological sense even though it denies God the great power that He has to form and reform all living things. The sages who commented on these stories over the years did not always agree with one another, or examine the tales from the same point of view. All their different interpretations, like the notes of a great symphony with apparent disharmonies, create together our conversation with the past.

Then there was the rabbi who scolded Leah for going out to Jacob and saying you are to sleep with me for I have hired you with my mandrakes. He said that such boldness turned her into a harlot, which is why her daughter went out to the fields and was raped. No question the rabbis did not like boldness in women, and many people believed and some believe to this day that the sins of the parents are redeemed by the misfortunes of the children.

And then at last God heard Rachel's prayers. She had waited a long time. She had suffered a long time. She must have almost abandoned hope. Her womb would not fulfil its purpose but remained closed, small like a fist within her, small like the pit of a dried fruit. But still she called on God to remember her, and one day He did. Was it the mandrake root that made the difference? Some would believe that. A root chopped and grated, mixed up with other herbs, this was sorcery, this was witchcraft. Others rejected the story. It was not the mandrake root. It was God who all along planned to grant Rachel a child. It was God who opened her womb and heard her plea, granting Rachel the gift of motherhood.

M. Avot said, "The more wives the more witchcraft." In other words the less a woman could determine the shape of her days the more she turned to oils and herbs, to potions and inventions of the dark art. Of course men have always been afraid of the secret powers of women and called them witches, when in truth their powers were small and their defeats numerous.

And so it was, one day Rachel realized that her time of the month had come and gone. One day she must have noticed that she felt weak in the morning and she could not eat without a surge of unpleasantness in her stomach. More days passed, and Tishri turned into Heshvan and Rachel had dark circles under her eyes. She slept little, thinking all night of how to keep the baby safe within her, let it grow.

Rachel grew full with child. Now she must have smiled at all she passed. Now her color was high, and she walked with a lightness in her step, despite her growing size, her expanding figure. God had heard her plea and answered her, rendering her a woman among other women, a creator of life, His servant on earth.

Some sages said that it was on the first day of the New Year, God heard the prayers of Jacob and Leah and Zilpah and Bilhah and Rachel herself and opened her womb. The sages were imagining a friendship among the women, a loyalty that surpassed rivalry, as they spoke to God in one voice for the sake of Rachel. Rabbi Hanina said that all the women of the camp prayed that Rachel would have a son, saying, "We have sufficient." That might have been so, or it might not. It would have been generous and virtuous of the women to wish Rachel such good fortune and to have counted themselves satisfied, but if such sisterhood existed there at the beginning of history would women not have ruled the world ever after?

Genesis 30:22, "And God remembered Rachel and God heard her and He opened her womb." Now it was Rachel's time. She lay down on the cloth that covered the bed pallet, and the midwife came to her side and wiped her brow with a cloth dipped in clear water from the well. Bilhah came to her side and sang songs of the field, of lambs and goats and hummingbirds singing. The pain was hard and it was long, but Rachel's joy was great and carried her aloft above the contractions, as if she were a bird high above a seething ocean. She remembered her mother's face, which she had last seen so long ago. The baby came in the usual pool of blood, covered with yellow wax, his mouth open to take in the air, his lungs full. He cried. It was a son. Genesis 30:23 she said, "God has taken away my shame." And she called his name Joseph, which is to say, "May the Lord add me another son." The name Joseph contains the root of the verb "to add."

Most of us at the birth of our first child are not thinking of the second. We are so overwhelmed with the experience, the pain, the exhaustion, the heart beating quickly that attends the child's entrance into the world, that we cannot think of the next. But Rachel had the example of her sister before her; one son would hardly stand up to six. Rachel could not rest in her good fortune but immediately asked God for another favor. How human of her—how understandable. How long she had waited, how patient she had been, how much she needed the child before her and the next one she would conceive.

Some rabbis have said that if she had not been so forward as to ask for a second son she might have had six more. But it's hard to believe that God would punish Rachel for a mere wish, one so easily understood. Nor was it likely that God would punish Rachel for wanting as many sons as her sister, so common was that urge, so natural to the human heart that God would have no time to do anything else if He punished every covetous thought that passed through a human mind.

Some sages say that Rebekah sent Deborah, her old nurse, to Paddan-aram to urge Jacob to return home to the land of his father. More likely it came to Jacob that he had served many years and had nothing of his own; all the livestock belonged to Laban, and all the servants and slaves belonged to Laban, and all the land belonged to Laban, and the wells were his, and the gold was his, and Jacob had no more than the air he could hold in his hands. And so after the birth of Joseph he said to Laban, Genesis 30:26, "Send me off that I may go to my place and to my land. Give me my wives and children, for whom I have served you, that I may go." And Laban said, Genesis 30:28, "Name me your wages that I may give them." Jacob did not want shekels. He did not want bits of pottery or trinkets of gold.

What he wanted was what he was owed, a portion of the wealth that had come to Laban through Jacob's hard labor.

Jacob said to Laban, Genesis 30:29, "You know how I have served you and how your livestock has fared with me. For the little you had before my time has swollen to a multitude and the Lord has blessed you on my count. And now when shall I, too, provide for my household." Jacob who had observed many sheep and many goats give birth had noticed carefully how the matter proceeded, and he asked Laban to give him the spotted and the speckled in the flock and to keep those that were pure white for himself, and in this way the flock would be separated into parts. Laban gave the dark and the speckled to his sons to guard and took the pure white of his flock, and allowed Jacob to watch over them. He rode away on a three-day journey with the speckled goats and the speckled sheep. And he was pleased with his cleverness because the white would not mate with the speckled, and there would be in the next birthing season many many more white than dark, and an agreement had been made, and Jacob would have to abide by it, taking what few he had from the flock.

But Jacob had his own plan. He took wet rods of poplar and almond and plane tree and peeled away the barks leaving white strips and he stood the rods in the troughs, in the water channels where the animals came to drink. And the beasts bore brindled, spotted, and speckled young. And he separated the weak from the strong and bred the strong again, using the rods, leaving the weak without sight of a speckled pole, and so the weak became all white and were to be given to Laban. His flock increased and his wealth increased, and he had male slaves and camels and donkeys.

In fact you can mate in a blue room and you will not have a blue baby; neither will your cat or dog or horse. Animals acquire certain traits not because of what they see but because of the spinning and melding, the miraculous dance of genes inside the embryo. But perhaps God was helping Jacob, saving him from his father-in-law, who was cunning without being good, while Jacob was cunning and good, or at least the hero of our story.

The sages said that angels came down each evening and brought Laban's flocks the three-day journey to those of Jacob and allowed them to mate before carrying them back before dawn. It is a wonderful thought, the skies full of flying sheep and goats and the soft hush of angel wings driving the herd through the wind, under the stars and the moon.

The sages said that Jacob had come to Laban with empty hands, and he left him with herds numbering six hundred thousand. Their increase had been amazing, an increase that will be equaled only when the Messiah comes. Robert Alter's translation of Genesis tells us in a footnote that the name Laban means "white," and so Jacob was beating his sly father-in-law with his own name.

Laban and his sons saw that Jacob had gathered a great flock, and they were angry. They muttered against him, and Jacob feared that they would do him harm in order to keep for themselves the wealth he had gained. Jacob called a meeting of his wives. He held the meeting in the middle of an open field so none of Laban's sons or his servants could hear the words spoken among the three of them. He told Rachel and Leah that their father was ill disposed toward him. He told them that he had worked hard for their father and that his wages had been switched ten times over. He told them that God had been with him and created kids and lambs, spotted, brindled, and speckled. And he told his wives that God had come to him in a dream and told him that He had formed the animals so that they would belong to Jacob because God had seen Laban's treachery. The Lord had said to Jacob in his dream, in Genesis 31:13–14, "Now, rise, leave this land, and return to the land of your birthplace." Jacob did not tell Leah and Rachel about his peeled rods or his skill as an animal breeder. He wanted them to know that God had been on his side, and if they left their father's camp, they would be accompanied by God on the journey.

Rachel and Leah may have talked together before this

meeting in the fields. They may have admitted to each other the bitter fact that their father had given both of them to Jacob in return for labor that would benefit him but would leave them without an inheritance, a dowry, a single camel, a single sheep, that would belong to their new lives. He used their worth for his own means. Perhaps Leah had been slower to realize that her father had betrayed her. It was a hard thing to accept, especially when the love of your husband is turned toward another. The two sisters sat silently. Leah must have known that Rachel was right. Rachel must have known that Leah was sad. She was sad too but would not hide from the truth.

And so the time came for the shearing of the flocks, and Laban traveled far with his sons and his male servants. There was a sudden silence in the camp. The camels remained. The household servants set about the washing and the brushing and the braiding and the weaving and the pounding of grain. Perhaps the very sky seemed to be holding its breath. The rains did not fall, washing away the blossoms on the fruit trees. The great leaves of the date palms hung listlessly. History was holding its breath.

Then when Jacob was certain that Laban was well off over the nearby hills and would not soon return he called to his men to prepare his flock. He called to his wives to come with the children, and he set the small ones on donkeys and he set his wives on camels. He sent his female and males slaves out on foot. All their possessions were wrapped in rugs and clothes and bundles and loaded on the camels. The tents themselves were set under the saddles.

*B*efore they left, Rachel went into the tent of her father. She must have smelled his smell in the closed air. She may have run her hands over his blankets or picked up his comb, the one he used to groom his beard. She may have put her hands on his extra boots still damp from some expedition to a far river. She saw his teraphim, his household gods, stone, dead eyed, on a stool. She picked them up and stuffed them under her shawl, holding the garment tight about her body with one hand, and with the other she grasped them as if they were jewels, jewels that belonged to her.

How is this possible, the beautiful and good Rachel, the compassionate Rachel, taking her father's household gods, who protect him and bring him good fortune as she leaves her home, the only home she has ever known? The rabbis wondered about this. One sage thinks that Rachel stole the household gods so that her father could no longer practice idiolatry. Maybe, but it seems likely that this form of idolatry was common and coexisted in many families with the love of the one true God. Was this theft actually to save her father from a theological mistake? It seems equally likely that Rachel wanted to take with her something of worth, something that would remind her of her childhood, something that she felt belonged to her even though she had not been given it. Rachel does not tell Jacob what she has done.

Other rabbis had said that Rachel stole the teraphim so that they would not reveal to Laban the exact location of Jacob's family. She must have told Leah. Remember, when tempted to condemn Rachel for this theft that the daughters of the house were given nothing of their own by a father who had profited from their marriages.

Here is another description of the oracle teraphim, found in Robert Graves and Raphael Patai's *Hebrew myths*: "They took a man who was the firstborn, slew him and took the hair off his head, then salted the head and anointed it with oil, then they wrote 'The name' upon a tablet of copper or gold and placed it under his tongue." The power of this teraphim lay in the power of the name of the God placed inside the head. It is unpleasant to think of Rachel, taking such a thing into her hands. Was it an act of courage to steal this repulsive object? One wonders if anyone buried the body of the man who was murdered to make the teraphim. Did anyone miss him? Was he a worthy man or an unworthy man? Why, if you looked at the most minor figures in the great tales, did you often see an open mouth in a silent scream that history would not hear? But perhaps the teraphim that Rachel stole were only clay or stone statues.

Jacob took his family across the Euphrates. Slowly they led the animals laden with goods, stumbling in the waters across to the other shore. Slowly the camels picked up their heavy hooves and sank into the mud of the riverbank. Slowly the women and the children carried on the backs of donkeys made their way across. On the other side the children splashed in the water, Leah and Rachel washed themselves in the clear running river.

The next day they traveled on toward Gilead. Meanwhile the shepherds of Haran saw that the well, which had been filled to overflowing since Jacob had arrived, ran dry suddenly. For three days they waited in hopes that the waters would return. Then they sent a messenger to Laban, who immediately knew that his daughters and his grandchildren had fled with their husband. Laban must have known that Jacob had deceived him as he had deceived his father. He must have gone to his tent to consult with his teraphim. He saw that they too were gone. He gathered all his kinsmen and in a great temper pursued Jacob.

For seven days they rode furiously, stopping barely to rest the animals and take water and food. Genesis 31:24 says, "And God came to Laban the Aramean in a night-dream and said to him, 'Watch yourself, lest you speak to Jacob either good or evil!'" The Holy One told Laban in his dream that he should not rebuke or harm Jacob at all. Then they found them. Jacob had made camp on the high hills in Gilead, and Laban and his armed men approached with their swords raised and with howls of war.

Leah and Rachel were afraid when they saw their father, flashing his sword, walking quickly toward them, followed by so many of his kin. They hid in their tent. The older boys had taken up swords and were waiting behind the tents should anyone harm the women. The servants too had crept out to hide in the bushes and were prepared to come to Jacob's aid in a moment.

Laban said to Jacob in a terrible voice, Genesis 31:26, "'What have you done, deceiving me and driving my daughters like captives of the sword? Why did you flee in stealth and de-

ceive me and not tell me? I would have sent you off with festive songs, with timbrel and lyre. And you did not let me kiss
my grandsons and daughters . . . and why did you steal my
gods?'" Jacob replied, "For I was afraid that you would rob
me of your daughters. With whomever you find your gods,
that person shall not live. Before our kinsmen claim what is
yours and take it.'" But Jacob did not know that Rachel, his
beloved, had stolen the teraphim, and it was her life he had
promised Laban.

Laban began to search. He must have turned over every
pot, he must have unwrapped every bundle in Jacob's tent. He
found nothing. He went through the servants' belongings. He
searched the bags on the camels and the rugs on the donkeys,
and he roared and he howled, and he called out to God to witness that he had been robbed and help him find the idol that
had comforted him often in the first light of dawn.

He went into the tents of the serving girls Bilhah and Zilpah
and he made them undress, in case they were hiding his property on their bodies. They stood before him naked and he
found nothing. He went into the tents of his grandsons. He
may have found a stick, or a collection of pebbles from the
river, a half-eaten plum, and a small trinket of gold hanging by
a thread on a bag. He did not find his teraphim. He went into
Leah's tent. He did not talk to her. She had betrayed him, and
he wanted nothing more to do with her. He would not have
looked at her, not even when she called his name in hopes of a
glance.

He went into Rachel's tent and there she was sitting on the
cushion she used when riding her camel. She had hidden the

teraphim under the cushion. Laban tore open her sack of clothes. He may have put his sword right through her bed cover. She said to him, in Genesis 31:35, "Let not my Lord be incensed that I am unable to rise before you, for the way of women is upon me." Perhaps Laban ripped open a silken cloth that she had hung at the opening of her tent. He left without saying a word. A woman at her time of the month was not to be touched by a man. Her sitting down before him while she was bleeding was permissible. The teraphim were not discovered. The rapid beating of her heart slowed down. Her life was not taken, not then.

Laban was obliged to respect her excuse because he was afraid of coming into contact with her while she menstruated. It was said that a man who passes between two menstruating women could fall dead. This attitude contributed to the separation of women in synagogues and mosques. The original reason was probably to prevent festive gatherings from becoming orgiastic, as they did among some cultures in the area.

Jacob unknowingly had cursed Rachel by threatening death to whomever had taken the teraphim. A curse cannot be revoked. It now hangs in the air like a sword over Rachel's head. A curse is a terrible thing and shows how long ago it began, this confusing of wish and fact, this fear of the spoken evil word, this outrageous mistaking of man's passion for the workings of fate.

Then Laban and Jacob made a pact not to invade or torment each other. They had a feast and they set up a pillar of stone marking the boundary between them. And Jacob swore to the agreement by "the terror of his father Isaac." He was a man who understood that his God was like a wild tiger; a man could only kneel before him. The marking of boundaries by stones was an old custom. A stone can so easily serve as a wall to separate people, and a wall can serve as a stone to mark the boundary, the end of one group's possession and the beginning of another's.

Jacob rose that night and led his two wives and his two slave girls and his eleven boys and his daughter as well as his slaves and servants and he crossed the Jabbok ford, a stream leading into the Jordan River. He sent a messenger to Esau, who lived in the mountains of Seir, which some said was the steppe leading to Eden. He had brought with him across the river oxen and donkeys and sheep and slaves that he intended to give to Esau as an offering in hopes that the brothers could abide in the same land in peace. The messenger returned, saying Esau was riding out to meet him with four hundred men. Jacob did not have such numbers. He was afraid.

Both sisters must have been afraid for their lives, afraid for their children. Would Esau make slaves of them all?

Legend tells us that Jacob placed Dinah in a box and covered the box with a cloth because he feared that Esau would demand marriage with her, as was his right as her uncle. Legend says that God then spoke to Jacob and said, "Since you have acted uncharitably toward your brother Esau, Dinah shall bear children to Job the Uzzite, no kinsman of yours! Moreover since you rebuffed a circumcised son of Abraham she shall yield her maidenhead to an uncircumcised Canaanite and since you denied her lawful wedlock, she shall be taken unlawfully."

Jacob split his people and his flocks in parts and sent the herdsmen ahead of him, saying that if they should meet Esau they should tell him that these flocks were a tribute from his brother Jacob. In this way he sought to soothe Esau's fury. He thought that if Esau should attack one group, the other might escape. He himself spent the night alone on the far side of the stream. An angel, or was it a demon, or was it the spirit of the outraged Esau, wrestled with Jacob that night, and it touched him in his hip socket and he was stung with a great pain. But at the first rays of dawn he had pinned the figure down, and he refused to let him go until he had been blessed. The spirit from another place then changed Jacob's name to Israel, saying, "You have striven with God and man, and won out."

Jacob crossed back to his waiting family. Rachel must have gone immediately to his side when she saw he was limping. He must have told of his struggle with the emissary of God. Perhaps he pulled his leg along the ground, leaning against his wife.

Jacob went out of his tent. In the distance he saw Esau approaching and with him were his battalion of men. Now Jacob placed the slave girls and their children first and Leah and her children after them and Rachel and Joseph last, where they would be the safest and have the longest time to run and hide. Leah must have understood her placement and was not surprised. Perhaps she allowed a small bitter smile to play across her lips. She no longer minded for herself, but surely she ached for her children. Jacob had shown that he valued Rachel's one child above her many. Rachel on the other hand may have longed to be at the side of her sister.

*T*here is a legend told in Robert Graves and Raphael Patai's book taken from the Sepher Hayashar that Laban sent his son Beor and his cousin Abilhoreph and ten others to Mount Seir to Esau to tell him Jacob was coming. Esau with his allies went forward, intending to destroy his brother, but one of Laban's messengers came to Rebekah and told her that Esau was moving against Jacob. She then sent seventy-two men who were of Isaac's camp to assist Jacob, and she said to the messenger, "Beg my son Jacob to show Esau the most obsequious humility and placate him with rich gifts and truthfully answer all his questions."

Jacob bowed down seven times as he approached Esau. His head touched the ground and he pulled himself up, one hip lit with pain as he moved it. The practice of bowing seven times as one approaches a monarch from a distance was common court ritual and found in documents from Amara and Ugaritic writings. Genesis 33:4, "And Esau ran to meet him and embraced and fell upon his neck, and they wept." And Jacob told Esau that the children that he saw were, Genesis 33:5, "the children that God had favored upon his servant." Esau embraced him and called him brother and graciously attempted to refuse the gifts of cattle and goods that Jacob had set aside for him, but Jacob said, "Pray take my blessing that has been brought you." Esau, who had become a wealthy prince even without the birthright, only reluctantly accepted his offerings. Esau wanted to ride back to his own home site with Jacob, but Jacob declined, making the excuse that his family and his herds needed time to make such a long journey.

As soon as Esau's men were out of sight, Jacob turned toward Succoth in the opposite direction of Seir. He did not trust his brother. Although Rachel and Leah may have both hoped that the true warmth of brother for brother could be rekindled, we have no word of that in Genesis.

Rachel and Leah and the entire camp followed Jacob to Shechem, and Jacob bought a parcel of land where he pitched his tents for a hundred kesitahs (weights in gold and silver). He set up an altar there. Rachel may have prayed at that altar for another son. Leah prayed at the altar that God watch over her sons and keep them from harm. Leah may have prayed at the altar that God would give her daughter Dinah a good husband who would cherish her above all others.

But perhaps she shouldn't have asked God for this thing. Because Dinah went out to the fields and was taken by Shechem, the son of Hamor prince of the land and he raped her. But then he felt love for her, great love that knew no bounds. Shechem asked his father, Hamor, to give him Dinah as a wife. His father went to Jacob to arrange a bride price. And Jacob's sons came in from the field when they heard this. The young men were very incensed because of the rape of their sister. Hamor hoped to form an alliance with Jacob and his sons through the marriage of his son with Dinah. The sons of Jacob now exercised their own deceit, their own trickery, and informed the prince that he and his sons and all his men must be circumcised if this mating were to occur. And the prince agreed, and all his male folk were circumcised in the hopes of including all of Jacob's possessions and livestock among their own.

On the third day, when the pain of circumcision is greatest, the day the angels visited Abraham after his circumcision, Leah's sons Simeon and Levi took up their swords and came upon the city unopposed, and they killed every male. And they slit the throats of Shechem and his father, and their blood ran down into the ground. The brothers looted the town of all its sheep and cattle and donkeys and all their wealth, and all their young ones and their wives they took captive. Then they took Dinah from the tent in which she had been held by Shechem.

The innocent were killed along with guilty. The punishment seemed more than the crime should have evoked. Many sages imagined the massacre of the Hivites—their children screaming and their wives weeping—and took pity on all who died that day. God too slaughtered every living soul (except Lot and his family) in the town of Sodom, and even before that He drowned most all the world in his mighty Flood. Massacre was not unknown to God.

Jacob, however, realized that others in the land would be angry with his people and might rise against them in numbers they could not defeat, and so he packed up his camps again and left.

Leah was proud of her sons. They had defended the honor of her daughter. She must have held the girl in her arms and consoled her for the fright, for the pain, for the taint that clung to her because she was no longer a virgin.

Rachel was with child again. She dared not think of the dead who had been neighbors. She dared not question the act of Leah's sons. But she may have been fearful that a terrrible event would befall them all because they had taken so much life. She might have heard the little children from the other tribe whispering in the distant tent, feverish with hurt and loss and trusting no longer in the good smell of the dirt or the sweet dates that were offered them.

It was a terrible thing that Dinah should have been taken, an innocent in the golden wheat. But retribution is rarely the end of the story, only the beginning of the next chapter. Think of Troy destroyed for the sake of Helen. There is a moral puzzle here that we deal with still. We are deeply troubled by collective punishment, since we hold individuals responsible for their own actions, and yet in the affairs between nations and groups it happens again and again.

God told Jacob to go to Bethel and live there and build an altar to God. Legend tells us that Jacob told his household to put away the alien gods that are in your midst and cleanse yourselves and change your garments. It seems that among the earliest of the followers of the one true God, some of the neighboring idols had been adopted. Now after all that bloodletting it was the time for purification, for atonement.

Likely Rachel did not want to part with her father's teraphim. But she did not want to disobey her husband either or her true God who had granted her prayer and allowed her to conceive once more. She put her hands on her rounded belly and felt the first fluttering of life within. Rachel may have taken her father's teraphim out by the stream under the deep green willow tree and put the stolen idols gently down in the water. They may have been carried by the current beyond the next bend in the shore and then have sunk down toward the mud.

Rachel would have prayed that this new child would be another boy.

And Jacob came to Bethel and God spoke to him and promised that a nation of kings would come from his loins, and Jacob set up a pillar of stone and poured oil on it. And slowly then they traveled onward, and when they were still some distance from Eprath, Rachel must have felt the wetness of her water on her thighs and the first of her pains. The camp stopped moving. The animals were left to graze on the land. Fires were built and blazed into the night. A celebration was planned. The women whispered among themselves. Perhaps a shooting star was seen in the sky. A good omen. Perhaps now Leah came to Rachel's side. She brought her water from her bowl. She helped the midwife who stroked her belly, pushing the baby downward. It was slow. The pains did not increase rapidly. They did not grow closer together. But they were strong, and the hours passed, and Rachel was exhausted. Her hair must have been damp with sweat. Her lips white. She would have taken deep breaths, as if the air itself was disappearing. The camp must have been quiet with expectation. But as the afternoon passed into night and the night passed into dawn, a somber silence would have fallen over the smallest child, even the slaves and the servants and the shepherds. Even the camels and the donkeys were still, as if they understood that a life, or maybe two lives, were suspended above them.

Genesis 35:17: "And it happened, when she was laboring hardest in the birth, that the midwife said to her, 'Fear not, for this one, too is a son for you.'" Leah grew so weary that she may have dropped into sleep while sitting at her sister's side. Leah may have startled awake in time to see Rachel no longer able to cry out.

Jacob must have known that all was not going well. He would have stood hour after hour right outside the tent, not daring to enter the women's domain. He may have prayed to God rudely, abruptly, desperately. His jaw must have ached and his head pounded. His manservant would have brought him water and bread, but he could not eat. Perhaps he sat down beneath a myrtle tree.

Now the baby was moving downward into the birth passage. It was nearly over, but Rachel's heart was growing faint. Her eyes were dim. Her head seemed to be splitting in two. Her arms flailed. She reached over and pulled Leah toward her. And the head appeared between Rachel's legs and the midwife pulled the baby forward, and he slid out of the canal. Perhaps Rachel was too exhausted to give thanks to the Lord for the birth of her second son. Genesis 35:18, "And it happened as her life ran out, for she was dying, that she called his name Ben-oni," which means "son of my vigor." But it could also mean "son of my sorrow."

Immediately on hearing the rustling and shouting from the women in the tent Jacob must have entered and seen his new son, his last son, stained with the blood of his mother, his cord still hanging from him, his mouth open in a cry of greeting to the world. Jacob must have gone to his beloved wife's side and seen that all was not well. Her face was white. Her hands were shaking and her legs were trembling and her chest heaved as she drew air inward. Perhaps Leah had not left her side. Jacob must have leaned down as Rachel searched for his face with her eyes, then she died.

Leah may have screamed. Jacob would have walked away silently. Only when he was away from the women would he have wept. And then his grief must have been as heavy as the mist on Mount Sinai.

Jacob renamed his son Benyamin, son of my right hand, meaning "favored son," or perhaps it meant "son of my old age." The sages believed Rachel was thirty-six years old at the time of her death.

It was not possible for Jacob to bury his beloved Rachel in the cave of Machpelah with Abraham and Sarah, with Rebekah and Isaac. They were too far away from Hebron to do this. It was not possible with his slow-moving caravan burdened by animals and small children and women to reach the cave in decent time. So Jacob buried Rachel on the road outside Eprath, which is now Bethlehem. Jacob set up a pillar on her grave. It was said that Rachel was buried on the roadside where centuries later her exiled people would walk on their long way to Babylon and that she wept for them as they passed by her, and she interceded with God, asking forgiveness for them and gaining a promise from Him that the people should return one day to the land.

A sage said that Rachel interceded with God for her exiled people. God was angry with Israel for worshiping other gods and intended the exile to be permanent, but Rachel said to Him, "If I could overcome my jealousy and tell Leah the signals that Jacob had given me, so surely you can forgive your people." And God granted her plea.

Jacob must have brought myrtle branches to place at the site, and he would have stayed there alone a long time. There must have been some hope in Leah's heart that now that Rachel was dead, she would become Jacob's love, his real wife. In this she was wrong. Nevertheless she mourned her sister. For the rest of her life she must have felt her absence, a shadow at her side, a memory that came every day, a presence of an absence that would have made her unlovely eyes close in pain.

When Benyamin learned to walk and began to talk, she would have told her sister, who could not hear. When they settled on the land and when her sons became warriors, she told Rachel. When Jacob came to her and talked of Rachel, which he did on the anniversary of her death and sometimes in between, she told Rachel, who could not hear. Perhaps she would rather have lost her husband than her sister, but the choice was not hers to make.

*J*ust as the willow withers before the other three species, so Rachel died before her sister," says Vayikra Rabba. The lovely willow, so dependent on rain and water running in the brook for its life, the willow with its thin branches and long leaves sends its seed out into the breeze but does not last in the heavy winds.

Some sages say that Rachel died as fulfillment of Jacob's promise to Laban that whoever had taken his teraphim would not live. Some say that Rachel died as a punishment to Jacob for his treachery to his brother. Some say that Rachel died because she took the mandrakes from her sister. Some say that Rachel died because she was envious of her sister's sons. That may be, but women died because the child was too slow in coming, because the child was twisted in the cord, because the heart of the child stopped beating or because a fever had come to the mother and infection had killed her. Perhaps it was Eve's sin that caused Rachel's death, or perhaps God has a plan that no man or woman will grasp until the end of time.

Legend says that during Rachel's lifetime her couch always stood in Jacob's tent. After her death he ordered the couch of her handmaiden Bilhah to be carried there. Reuben was angry because he knew that his mother would be pierced to the heart once again. He went and took the couch of his mother and placed it in Jacob's tent and removed that of the handmaiden.

It is said that Reuben repented of this bold act and Jacob forgave him and God forgave him. Of course it was also said that Reuben took Bilhah for his own woman, which would have been a deep outrage to his father, and close to incest. It is hard to know, looking so far back, who was the one who crossed the line and which line. What is clear is that Leah, who lived many more years and saw her sons grow strong and powerful, never was taken into Jacob's tent, although he treated her with respect due the mother of his offspring. Perhaps at the end we may hope that he felt a glimmer of friendship, a touch of affection for a lifetime partner, albeit one forced upon him.

It was said by some sages that Leah grew more beautiful as the years went by. Her hair turned white like the clouds but her face took on a wondrous look of strength, and her face reflected all the beauty of the seasons. It was said that her eyes became clear and her features pleasing, and her sons respected her and her servants loved her and God never abandoned her but watched over her always, keeping away snakes and harmful berries, keeping violence and trouble away from her tent. Perhaps.

Eighteen years after Rachel's death Leah herself died and was buried in the cave at Machpelah. All her sons wore sackcloth and ashes and the angels wept.

Some say that Esau and his sons came to attack Jacob that day because Isaac, who had asked them to live in peace with each other, had also died. Some say that Jacob killed Esau with an arrow that pierced his breast. But these are rumors that stand in the empty places where history is mute.

❧

And in the story of Leah and Rachel, the twelve tribes, founded one by one by each of Jacob's sons, begin their march toward Sinai, where they will receive the Ten Commandments, and the struggle of man with his cruel instincts will continue. The plot like the mind of a growing child brings ever more twists and turns as the centuries replace one another.

Long ago before the second destruction of the Temple a writer inscribed these words on a clay tablet.

> The world is like a human eye.
> The white is the ocean
> The iris is the earth
> The pupil is Jerusalem
> And the image therein is
> The temple of the Lord.

And if the world is an eye, then the world is watching God, eager to catch the smallest reflection of his will, rejoicing in the least sign of his attention. And the sisters Rachel and Leah stand there at the beginning of the tale, a tale full of peril, full of hope, passing their days embracing the love or lack of love that haunts us all. Rachel and Leah, Leah and Rachel, one whose love was returned and one whose love was rejected, are braided together throughout their lives. One suffered from barrenness and the other suffered from neglect. One had joy from children and one died in childbirth. Their grief, their disappointments, all under the God-filled sky, like ours, are the staples of female life. Woe and joy, joy and woe, hand in hand, how little is new, how little is different, now that we can almost send rockets up to God's throne. In the fullness of time, the hours pass in the making of food, the cleaning of cloth, the folding and opening, the peeling and mashing, the wiping, the nursing of infants, the washing of children, the holding and letting go, the days of sickness and health, amid the strange odors of beast and human, amid ripeness and decay, amid the sweet odors of flower and fruit.

Rachel and Leah—Leah and Rachel—their lives passed by so long ago and yet so clearly mark the present, telling the nation of its small beginnings, and God's central role in human affairs, reminding us that this maze of love and envy, war and deceit, betrayal and courage, has no exit.

Where They Are Buried

Rachel

RACHEL'S TOMB IS approached through a long gray cement hut-shaped structure attached to the old tomb site. It was built by the Israeli government for the protection of worshippers. At first it had windows that let in the light, but the Arabs shot at the Jews through the windows, so now they are blocked with protective metal, and one walks toward the ancient grave through a tunnel with a dim electric bulb lighting the way. There is a stone fountain for hand washing at the entrance just inside the metal door, which is guarded by a pair of soldiers and locked or opened by one of them. You walk through to the tomb site itself into a small room with a domed roof. The men—black hats, long beards, tallith fringes under their white shirts—are praying aloud, wailing, moaning, the rough sweet cry of human pain sifts through the praise of the deity; the women are silent. The men's prayers are interrupted when the rocks of emotion crash against one another as someone blows the shofar, whose piercing sound floats over into the women's side of the grave site.

You can see the men enter the area and disappear through another entrance. The women have their hair covered either with wigs or scarfs. The women's side of the room is separated from the men's by a high screen covered with a white cloth on which twelve circles have been simply embroidered, each including the symbol of a specific tribe.

The prayer books are in a small crowded shelf, and there are a few chairs in the room, but the women stand and I see tears in their eyes as they pray—one woman's hands are closed into fists and she rocks back and forth on her feet. The women are young, praying for conception, or old, praying for the health of someone they love. The room is very warm, and there is a musty odor of dust and sweat. "I am not praying to Rachel," said one Modern Orthodox American woman from the settlement of Efrat. "I am praying near her for my sister-in-law who has just been diagnosed with cancer." Standing there it is impossible not to absorb the suffering that the prayers reveal. A person's heart could break from the intensity, from the desperation, from the hope they express in divine mercy.

With a guide with a rifle carried on his shoulder, with a driver who keeps his rifle beside him, we have driven to Bethlehem in an armored van. The bulletproof windows are dim and doubled so I have trouble seeing the olive groves and can barely see the Arab men walking along with carts pulled by donkeys. We have stopped at a checkpoint and transferred to an army bus with four very young soldiers who carry rifles and sit in the front seats.

As I stand near the screen on the female side of the tomb an old bent woman takes a skein of red yarn out of her black bag and ties it to the post on one end of the screen and weaves it around the eight or nine women who are standing pressed up against the curtain. She ties the other end of the yarn to the other side of the screen and then cuts it free and into many little pieces. Each of the women take a piece from her. She hands me two pieces. The red yarn is to keep away the evil eye, a teraph in fabric form perhaps. Here in the presence of Rachel it is possible that the evil eye redoubles its efforts or we must redouble our efforts against it.

Is Rachel weeping for her children at the tomb site? Is she interceding with God for us in our collective and individual suffering? Is this even the actual burial place of her body? Some say she was buried up north on the road to Babylon so the battered and defeated Jews would pass by her grave on their way to exile, not here in what once was the outskirts of Bethlehem and now seems to be on a busy street on which children walk on their way to school and an Arab man carries a package from the grocery store on the corner, walking past the Israeli soldiers without lifting his eyes from the ground.

It does say in Genesis that she was buried on the way to Bethlehem while Jacob was traveling to Hebron. But is her body really here? Does it matter? What is true is that the women gathered in the small room believe that the space they are standing in is immersed in the sacred, that they themselves will be touched by God at this place.

To one side of the small room there is a wall hanging made of two sand-colored panels of fine satin with gold threads running through it and a central panel of shining white silk. This fabric has been cut from Navah Applebaum's wedding dress and was donated to Rachel's tomb by her mother. In 2003 Navah Applebaum was killed in Jerusalem by a Palestinian suicide bomber the night before her wedding while having coffee in a café with her father, a doctor at Hadassah hospital, who died at her side.

Could any soul be unresponsive to the glistening panel made of Navah Applebaum's never-to-be-worn wedding dress? Anger rises at the sight. Grief doubles and doubles again. It seems that Rachel may weep for her children but she cannot stop the mayhem and the slaughter.

A bus comes every Tuesday morning from the Efrat settlement to the tomb so that the women can pray. They come to establish that Jews can and will attend the grave of their beloved Rachel. They come to say that the presence of this grave in Bethlehem gives the Jews the historical right to the land in which their ancestor is buried. This part of their visit is a political statement infused with religious conviction. God gave this land to us, and we were here first, they announce by arriving week after week in armored buses. These women take claim to the tomb by their presence at it. But their prayers are not national. They are deeply personal. You can see this in the tears in the eyes, in the drawn faces, in the white fingers holding the prayer books. You can see it in the hunch of backs, in the tightness around the mouth. You can feel it in the air, all the terrible events that beset us, young and old, no matter how good or decent or God-fearing we are.

The women's section is earnest and unadorned, but the closed eyes of the worshippers, the silent turning of pages of prayer books, the peculiar wash of an almost weeping sound from the other side of the screen silences the rational mind.

The needs of the petitioners are almost tangible, as if they were objects floating here and there in the room as the worshippers wander in and out.

The walls are cold gray stone. The curtain and the bookshelves are shabby and more reminiscent of a shul in the small towns of the Pale than of the grand and glistening synagogues of America. The women wear socks and flat shoes and long skirts and no makeup. They have unfashionable hats or berets on their heads. Some wear tightly tied scarves. We are as far from the boutiques of Paris as a body can get. But of course, the need for the consolation and intervention of the Divine is the same on the Rue de Rivoli as it is on Fifth Avenue or in Bethlehem. This is as it always has been.

The women from Efrat go downstairs to a narrow basement room with plastic chairs where they study a story by Rabbi Nachman with a male rabbi who tells them that the meaning of the story is that God's face is in the world if they just look for it. Young soldiers, boys who should be playing soccer on a school field, pass through the little room, again and again, opening and closing the door that leads into an area off limits for visitors. The hard metal of their rifles clangs against the door as they open and close it. The nation too has need of Rachel's prayers.

It is a strange matter, this praying at the grave site of a Matriarch whose body may or may not be there, whose neurons and synapses turned to dust some three thousand years ago, if in fact her existence was actual and not merely fabled. It is true that Rachel's descendants, when praying for the sick, always offer the prayer through their mothers, reciting their mothers' names.

Is Rachel present in some way at her tomb? Certainly the will of the seekers, the wish of the seekers, the helplessness of the seekers before the violence of nature and the cruelty of man bring a rich sanctity to the tomb. God may not be a good listener. Rachel may not be a spirit hovering near to catch the whisperings of her petitioners, but surely the space is holy, holy because of the mountains of human want that have been released into that air, and surely God is present there if only in the prayers of praise and of entreaty that rise above the soldiers' heads and go wherever human prayers go, carrying our desolation and our hope.

Abraham and Sarah,
Jacob and Rebekah,
Isaac and Leah

*T*HERE ARE FEW cars on the road as we approach Hebron. A man works in an olive grove, and the stones of the terraced field are as gray as the sky. The road winds through the high hills of Judea, scrub and sand, brush and an occasional orange grove on the rocky cliffs. There the soldiers guard a checkpoint at one of the roads that leads off the main one. There is a long backup of cars waiting. The road winds higher, past the Jewish settlement in Hebron—small, fenced-in with high wires—and suddenly there is a street and houses in need of painting, and cobblestone roads with occasional flowers spilling out from high terraces. Down the hill is a group of young boys in white shirts and black pants, wearing wide black-brimmed hats beneath which come sweet curls down to their shoulders. Their hats seem large for their small heads. The boys are walking slowly. The threads of their prayer shawls hang from beneath their shirts. An Arab leading an extremely old and frail donkey pulling a cart with logs on it moves to the side as we pass. Soon we are in a plaza, in front of a structure of gray-white stone, washed with time and sun and weather. Here is the summer palace of Herod. He built it above the cave of Machpelah, which Abraham purchased as a burial site for Sarah from a man named Edom in the middle of the third millennium before the Common Era. Before moving to Jerusalem King David ruled for seven years from his palace in Hebron: perhaps it was nearby. It has been said that this is the entrance to the lower heaven where the Garden of Eden can be found guarded by two angels with swords of fire. The courtyard contains a dozen or so Israeli soldiers, milling about and talking, smoking, and watching us out of the corners of their eyes. We cross the plaza and go up a flight of stone steps and can see the houses on the hill beyond, from which shots have been fired at visitors to the grave sites, snipers with their rifles aimed at pilgrims and tourists. We go to a checkpoint where we pass through metal detectors and then go up the steps into the stone building where the Crusaders made their own shrine to Jesus in their own time. I open my pocketbook for inspection. The young Israeli soldier takes a compact with a mirror and promises to return it when we leave. She will not smile at me.

We enter an upper courtyard where there is a central open area, covered by a canvas cloth. There is an ark holding a Torah at one end of the improvised house of worship. We are protected from the sun. A few men with white beards are praying in their seats. A young boy of bar mitzvah age is going over a page in a large book with an old man by his side whispering in his ear. There are chairs set up as if for a service, but for now the room is almost empty. The air is hot, and heavy. There are soldiers in the corners and soldiers wandering around. Their boots can be heard on the steps. They are young but their eyes are stern.

To the left is the room that houses the tomb of Isaac and Rebekah. We can't go there. It has been closed to Jews by the Muslims ever since Baruch Goldstein shot and killed men at prayer, on their knees facing the tomb. How could anyone believe that God is pleased with this slaughter, here beside the tombs of those who knew Him first, those who heard His voice, those whose story is told again and again? How exactly does love of God grow into hatred for one's neighbor? Are we such beasts?

Or is it God's fault for not allowing all the people to build a tower to the skies and together presume on the realm of heaven?

We can go see Abraham's and Sarah's tombs, which are in a small room off the central courtyard. There are gold grates with decorative disks placed between the bars on either side of the room, and the tombs themselves, one on each side, are behind the locked gates. The tombs are large bread-loaf-shaped objects covered in a green or red tapestry with gold threads forming diamond patterns on the mound. In the little room there is an arc and a bookshelf with prayer books and a small chair behind a wooden screen where women can sit and pray. Visitors have written notes and dropped them on the rugs woven with diamonds and squares and vines twirling round and round. On the floor behind the grates, little pieces of paper lie like litter, but not litter. These contain the needs, the hopes, the cries of those who believe that in this special place God will heed their words, that Abraham and Sarah will open God's ears to their human pain. The notes are folded over; one cannot read the words. They are not meant for the eyes of strangers.

In the center of the little room is a table for the Torah when it is taken out of the ark. There are notes pressed between the bars and left on the worn carpets beside each of the tombs. Not many notes, not many visitors, on the Tuesday morning I arrive. On the other side of the courtyard is another identical small room holding the tombs of Jacob and Leah. Also in two separate grated cages. Large tombs, Arabic writing, green tapestries, and more notes scattered on the carpet beneath. There is another ark and another table attached to a small wooden panel to screen off women who may come to pray. There is no one else visiting beside me.

The bodies of course are most probably not in the tombs. The bodies might be below in the cave of Machpelah, deep inside the earth. When the Jews took Hebron in 1967 they tied a rope around a little girl and sent her down a small opening they found at the top of the structure. She went down as far as she could, and when they pulled her up she had in her hands some pottery shards that looked as if they could be burial artifacts, but before further exploration could be undertaken the Muslims sealed off the hole with cement. They did not want such absolute confirmation that Abraham had bought the land for the caves, establishing a Jewish claim to Hebron.

A few soldiers stood about with nothing to do. Herod used thick stones to build his palace, and his steps are steep, as if made for a larger people than we have become. The Israelis control the tombs now but they are surrounded by those who wish them gone, those who if they could, would deny them the right to pray at the tomb of their ancestors. How did it come to this? Isaac and Ishmael came together as brothers at the burial of their father, Abraham. They should never have been separated. But they were. What an irony here that now Jews and Arabs cannot even pray safely without a partition between them.

I sit down in a small chair outside the little room that holds Abraham's and Sarah's tombs. As I peer through the metal bars of the protective cage I catch a flash of a Kaffir, an Arab face on the other side, at prayer. We can see each other but we cannot touch. He quickly pulls back out of sight. Abraham is his father too. Is this Sarah's fault for insisting that Ishmael be cast out so the inheritance would belong to her son alone?

It does not matter to me if the dust of our progenitors is actually contained within these mounds. Because these souls were special, unique among humans for their role in our history and their importance to the people they created from their seed, and I am close to them from knowing their stories, a closeness of spirit that is far more satisfying than actually walking near the burial site. We the multiplied, the ones who are like stars in the sky or dust in the dirt, do we feel a reflection of God's covenant when we stand there, a kind of heat that draws us in, distracts us from the spinning of the globe, that will soon enough sweep us away to our own less substantial, mostly unvisited, grave sites?

The tombs are awesome in their size, awesome in the strange quiet that surrounds them. Behind their iron floor-to-ceiling grates are the dead, holy personages without life, but with a claim on eternity. What I feel is desire, desire to reach through the grates and touch the tombs, to stroke them tenderly. What I feel is a curious fear. The tombs are so large, like the shapes in a nightmare that have lost their edges, like eggs housing some monstrous being that will be hatched during the next full moon. There is a sign on the wall in Hebrew with a prayer written on it. The wooden frame around the sign is chipped, and the rug on the floor is threadbare. There is no attempt here to impress with the gold of empire, or the silver of worldly power. Although these are sacophagi, this is the anti-Vatican. Here the sacred is relatively unadorned. The bones are hidden. The dead are here behind gates waiting for visitors, admirers, friends, attention from the folk. Herod and the Crusaders have vanished, leaving behind nothing but stones. The shrine the Crusaders built at this spot no longer exists. But far down under my feet, Abraham, grieving for Sarah, whom he probably killed with his near sacrifice of Isaac, had wrapped his wife in her shroud and let the darkness have her. Even if it didn't happen, not like that, even if this was only a story, I want to pay my respects, mark my visit, approach God, approach my ancestors, see Sarah folding clothes in the desert dust. But the dead are dead and the tomb holds only ashes, and whose ashes I don't know.

*I*t would be easier to think of God without the soldiers all around. There is a watchtower up to the left of the courtyard. A rifle is pushed through the opening in the arch; I see the black metal shining in the sun. I see the forearm of a soldier. I see the pale smoke of his cigarette as it ascends toward the clouds, drifts toward the Arab houses across the way. But here, the soldiers, secular or religious, make it possible for us to walk up the stone stairs, through the stone corridors, and up onto the burial site, the Jewish side, that is.

Many religions have their sacred places. There is Lourdes and there is the hadj, the place where Muhammad saw God, and there is the Temple Mount, where he rode off to heaven mounted on his horse. There is the river Ganges, where the gods spilled the elixer of immortality while fighting with one another. There are pilgrimages to the place where Christ was born and the place he was said to breathe his last, nails in his hands and feet. We turn our world into a map of sites where things of God have been said to have come to pass. We feel less alone that way.

I too want to leave something of myself at the tombs. I crumple a small old photograph of my children that I keep in my notebook and slip it through the bars outside of Jacob's and Leah's tombs. As God held Abraham and Sarah, Isaac and Rebekah, Jacob and Rachel and Leah in his sight, may he do so with my children, I whisper. Maybe he will.

*S*arah, Rebekah, Rachel, and Leah were not altogether good women. They each had failings, moments that marked them as less than saints, more real and more human than any ideal could be. If these imperfect women could serve so great a purpose then we, who are also morally frail, can too. Because of their stories we can forgive ourselves our own jealousy, distrust, and acts of bad faith and continue to strive to be decent people, knit together in the hope that our lives can in small ways better the world or at least keep it spinning on its axis.

*I*t is the sweaty soldiers guarding the sacred site who are the reality here, the only certain facts I find. And yet as I go down the steps and head toward the armored van that will take me away from Hebron and all its hatreds and dangers and shabby buildings I am urgently pressed to say thank you, thank you to the white bearded man who floats about the courtyard, handing me a card with his Web site describing the tombs, or the young Jewish soldier, Ethiopian I guess, from the shining black of her skin, who returns my compact, or the driver of my van, or my guide, who helps me up the step into the seat, or the long line of story and history and prayer that marks this spot, marks it for worship, marks it for trouble, marks it for bloodshed, marks it for mystery. What will the end of the story be?

BIBLIOGRAPHY

Abrams, Judith Z. *The Women of the Talmud*. Northvale, N.J.: Jason Aronson Inc., 1995.

Alter, Robert, trans. *Genesis*. New York: W. W. Norton, 1996.

———. *The Five Books of Moses*. New York: W. W. Norton, 2004.

Asimov, Isaac. *Words in Genesis*. Boston, Mass.: Houghton Mifflin, 1962.

Baskin, Judith. *Midrashic Woman: Formations of the Feminine in Rabbinic Literature*. Hanover, N.H.: Brandeis University Press, 2002.

Bialik, Haymin Nahman, and Yehoshua Hana Ravnitsky, eds. *Book of Legends*. New York: Schocken Books, 1992.

Bloom, Harold. *The Bible (Bloom's Modern Critical Views.)* New York: Chelsea House Publications, 2000.

Bokson, Ben Zion, trans. *Selected Writings of the Talmud.* New Jersey: Paulist Press, 1989.

Cahill, Thomas. *The Gifts of the Jews.* New York: Doubleday, 1998.

Cohen, A., ed. *The Soncino Chumash, Vol.1.* London: The Soncino Press, 1983.

Cohen, Victor. *The Soul of the Torah: Insights in Chasidic Masters on the Weekly Torah Portions.* Northvale, N.J.: Jason Aronson Inc., 2000.

Darom, David. *Beautiful Plants of the Bible, From the Hyssop to the Mighty Cedar Trees.* Herzlia, Israel: Palphot Ltd.

Etz Hayim. New York: The Rabbinical Assembly, 2001.

Feiler, Bruce. *Walking the Bible: A Journey by Land Through the Five Books of Moses.* New York: William Morrow, 2001.

————. *Abraham: A Journey to the Heart of Three Faiths.* New York: William Morrow, 2002.

Freedman, H., Maurice Simon, and E. London. *The Midrash.* London: Soncino Press, 1951.

Ginzberg, Louis, and Henrietta Szold, trans. *Legends of the Jews. Vol 1*. Philadelphia: Jewish Publication Society, 1909.

Glatt, Rabbi Aaron Eli. *Women in the Talmud*. Brooklyn, N.Y.: Mesorah Publications, 2003.

Goldstein, Elyse Rabbi. *Revisions: Seeing Torah Through a Feminist Lens*. Woodstock, N.Y.: Jewish Lights, 2001.

Graves, Robert, and Raphael Patai. *Hebrew Myths: The Book of Genesis*. New York: McGraw-Hill, 1963.

Greenberg, Rabbi Irving. *The Jewish Way: Living the Holidays*. New York: Summit Books, 1988.

Hareuveni, Nogah, and Helen Frenkley, trans. *Nature in Our Biblical Heritage*. Kiryat Ono, Israel: Neot Kedumim Ltd., 1980.

Herson, Paul Isaac, trans. *A Rabbinical Commentary on Genesis*. London: Hodder and Stoughton, 1885.

Holtz, Barry W. *Finding Our Way: Jewish Texts and the Lives We Lead Today*. New York: Schocken Books, 1990.

Hyman, Naomi M. *Biblical Women in the Midrash*. Northvale, N.J.: Jason Aronson Inc., 1998.

Kensky, Tikva Frymer. *Reading the Women of the Bible*. New York: Schocken Books, 2002.

Kierkegaard, Søren. *Fear and Trembling*. New York: Penguin Books, 1985 (1843).

Klagsbrun, Francine. *Voices of Wisdom*. New York: Pantheon, 1980.

Konner, Melvin. *Unsettled: An Anthropology of the Jews*. New York: Viking Compass, 2003.

Linetsky, Michael. *Rabbi Abraham Ibm Exra's Commentary on the Creation*. Northvale, N.J.: Jason Aronson, 1998.

Moscati, Sabatino. *Ancient Semitic Civilizations*. New York: Putnam, 1959.

Nachshoni, Yehuda, and Himelstein Shmuel, trans. *Studies in the Weekly Parshah*. Brooklyn, N.Y.: Mesorah Publications, Ltd., 1988.

Newman, Aryeh, and Leibowitz Nehama, trans. *Studies in Bereshit*. New York: World Zionist Organization, 1974.

Pavlov, Rebbitzen Holly. *Mirrors of Our Lives: Reflections of Women in the Tanach*. Southfield, Mich.: Targum Press, Inc., 2000.

Reimer, Gail Twersky, and Judith A. Kates. *Beginning Anew: A Woman's Companion to the High Holy Days*. New York: Touchstone Press, 1997.

Rosenbaum and Silberman. *Pentateuch with Rashi's Commentary*. New York: Hebrew Publishing Company.

Rubin, Gail. *Psalmist with a Camera*. New York: Abbeville Press, 1979.

Ruether, Rosmary Radford, ed. *Religions and Sexism: Images of Woman in the Jewish and Christian Traditions*. New York: Simon and Schuster, 1974.

Sarna, N. M. *Understanding Genesis*. New York: Schocken Books, 1970.

Sarna, Nahum, and Chaim Potok. *The JPS Torah Commentary: Genesis*. Philadelphia: The Jewish Publication Society, 1989.

Scherman, Rabbi Nosson. *The Stone Edition: The Chumash*. Brooklyn, N.Y.: The Art Scroll Series, Mesorah Publichations, 1993.

Sperling, Henry, and London and Maurice Simon, trans. *The Zohar*. London: The Soncino Press, 1931.

Steinsaltz, Adin, Hanegbi Yehuda, and Yehudit Keshet, trans. *Biblical Images: Men and Women of the Book*. New York: Basic Books Inc., 1984.

Valler, Shulamit, and Rozen Betty Sigler, trans. *Women and Womanhood in the Talmud*. Rhode Island: Brown Judaic Studies.

Wiesel, Elie. *Wise Men and Their Tales: Portraits of Biblical, Talmudic and Hasidic Masters*. New York: Schocken Books, 2003.

Zornberg, Aviva Gottleib. *Genesis: The Beginning of Desire*. Philadelphia: The Jewish Publication Society, 1995.